NICK ENRIGHT trained for the theatre on an Australia
Council grant at New York University School of the Arts and
studied playwriting with Israel Horovitz. His plays include *On the
Wallaby, Daylight Saving, St James Infirmary, Mongrels, A Property of
the Clan, Good Works, Playgrounds, The Quartet from Rigoletto,* and
Blackrock. With composer Terence Clarke he wrote *The Venetian
Twins, Variations* and *Summer Rain.* With Max Lambert he
collaborated on *Miracle City.* He adapted Dorothy Hewett's
Bobbin Up for NIDA. Nick has written for radio *Watching over
Israel),* television (*Come in Spinner* and *Coral Island–Naked* series)
and film (*Lorenzo's Oil,* with George Miller). His children's book
with Victoria Roberts, *The Maitland and Morpeth String Quartet,* has
been adapted for radio and made into an animated film. *Daylight
Saving* and *A Property of the Clan* won the Australian Writers'
Guild Gold Awgies in 1990 and 1993, and *Good Works* won the
Melbourne Green Room Award for best play in 1995.

Blackrock

Original Screenplay by
Nick Enright

Currency Press • Sydney

First published 1997 by
Currency Press Ltd,
PO Box 452, Paddington,
NSW 2021, Australia

10 9 8 7 6 5 4 3 2 1 0

NATIONAL LIBRARY OF AUSTRALIA CIP DATA
Enright, Nicholas, 1950-.
     Blackrock: the screen play.

     ISBN 0 86819 531 6

     1. Blackrock (Motion picture). I. Title. (Series: Currency screen plays).

     A822.3

Printed by Southwood Press, Marrickville NSW, Australia
Cover photograph: Simon Lyndon as Ricko and Laurence Breuls as Jared.
Photo: Elise Lockwood.

Contents

From Stage Play To Screenplay

Nick Enright

This screenplay began life in a very different form, as a play for young people commissioned by Freewheels, a Newcastle-based theatre company. In 1991 its director Brian Joyce invited me to write for the company. When asked to suggest a subject he mentioned the 1989 rape and murder of a young girl, Leigh Leigh, at a beach party, explaining that his concern was not with those horrible crimes but with the responses of the dead girl's peers to the events and their aftermath. Out of this and other discussions and interviews emerged a play called *A Property of the Clan*, the story of a young man, Jared, who witnesses a rape and fails to act.

Two years later, the Sydney Theatre Company asked me to develop the material into a play appropriate for their larger resources and wider audience. I jettisoned most of the original text, but kept its central triad of characters, Jared, his mother Diane and his best mate Ricko, together with Jared's girlfriend Rachel; and under the dramaturgical guidance of Wayne Harrison, David Berthold and an astute group of actors, I reworked the original narrative. The first draft of Blackrock was an epic affair nearly twice as long as the play which opened at the Wharf in 1995; but the discarded material became deep background for the screenplay you are now holding.

My old friend and colleague Steve Vidler, after more than a decade as an actor, had recently emerged from film school, and was searching for a project. Though nervous about the notion of plays becoming movies, I reminded him of *A Property of the Clan* and invited him to join us for the first STC workshop of the new play. He agreed that there might be a film in the material, and we went to work on a screenplay which we developed in tandem with the piece for the stage. David Elfick, when approached as prospective producer, shared Steve's enthusiasm for the story, and had insights of his own to offer. On our behalf he approached the NSW Film and TV Office for money to develop the screenplay. Their response was immediate and positive; indeed their support and encouragement throughout the project has been greatly valued.

On a tight budget and a rigorous schedule [six weeks from the end of August 1996], Steve and cinematographer Martin McGrath and their team managed to shoot every page of a complex [in some ways, as we discovered, over-complex] script. You will find that this published text includes every scene that was shot. In editing we found the film needed simplification, particularly-as so often happens-in its first twenty minutes. After the film's first screening at the Sundance Festival in January 1997, further cuts were made, all with my agreement, and some at my suggestion. All cuts are indicated in this text.

Most of my work is in the theatre; I have worked only rarely in film and television. This project had for me the best aspects of a collaboration in the theatre, a strong sense of ensemble and a shared focus on the text, together with the excitement and challenge of telling a story in images on a screen. However our film is ultimately judged, its strengths and weaknesses are our collective responsibility, for I believe the finished picture is substantially the one we set out to make. I thank David and Steve and Martin, Catherine Knapman, David McKay, Frans Vandenburg, Steve Kilbey, Charles Rotherham and all their cohorts. I offer special thanks to Christine King, who cast the film with such skill and sensitivity; and of course to the actors themselves; Linda Cropper, Laurence Breuls and Simon Lyndon and rest of the splendid ensemble cast.

Sydney, April 1997

The Gift of a Script

Steve Vidler

I could have been making a road movie. David Elfick and I had been working on what seemed like a sensible first film for me to direct–a rock'n'roll road movie that a young first-time writer had brought to him. Despite an enormous amount of work and from all parties concerned, as sometimes happens, things just fell apart. We all wanted to make a different movie–and no one with money to spend, it seemed, wanted us to make the movie at all. We all went our separate ways.

So I approached Nick Enright, whom I had known since our days at NIDA, and made him an offer he couldn't refuse. He would write a script, for about a tenth of his going rate, hand it over to me to direct, and if it ever got up, (which was unlikely, given my total lack of a track record), there was a fair chance I would screw it up anyway. How could he resist? In an act of faith, generosity or possibly just plain insanity, Nick said yes. He offered to write a film version of *Blackrock*.

I had first become aware of this story when I saw it in its incarnation as the community theatre piece, *A Property of the Clan*, at a test run for the education department in the hall of a Sydney high school. My first response at the time was 'this ought to be a film'. It was a powerful dramatisation of important issues-the first truly honest examination of the dark side of mateship I had seen-but let's face it, kids don't go to the theatre. Little did I realise I would ultimately be asked to put my money where my mouth was, and actually make the film.

I was immediately attracted to the idea, because I believe at some level we are all Jared. By this I mean that in this ever-shrinking global village we deal daily with issues of enormous moral complexity, and we are all tempted at times to turn our back or live in silent acquiescence. This story confronts us with an unsettling reflection of ourselves, yet ultimately offers hope that we can exercise our power to resist, and ultimately-even through the smallest action-make a difference.

Over a period of close to two years, we developed the screenplay in tandem with the play, a process aided in no little part by the contributions of the actors engaged in the many readings of the various drafts along the way. For this I thank them. I should also make mention here of Nick Enright's extraordinary lack of preciousness about his own work. Constantly in search of the best way to serve the story, right up to and including the final cut of the release print of the film, Nick was his own most demanding critic, deleting and altering scenes, never falling in love with a moment for its own sake, but constantly questioning its contribution to the whole.

Not too many first-time directors are blessed with the opportunity of working on a script by a writer whose last outing was nominated for an academy award. Nick Enright gave me the gift of a script that was emotionally compelling and joltingly relevant. I am proud to have been involved with him in the process of developing this screenplay, and proud of the film that has ultimately been realised.

Sydney, April 1997

How the script relates to the film

The script published here is the final shooting script. The following excerpts (from *Dead Heart* by Nick Parsons), show how differences in the finished film are noted. Other changes are mentioned in the text.

1. The scene numbers on the left are the original numbers in the shooting script. Bracketed numbers on the right, indicate the actual position of the scene in the film.

SCENE 120 EXT. THE AIRSTRIP – WALA WALA. DAY.   {121}

2. The * symbol indicates that in the film the particular scene formed only part of the finished scene. Thus Scenes 61 & 62 each form part of Scene 63.

SCENE 61   INT. THE KITCHEN – THE DOCTOR'S RESIDENCE.
NIGHT.   {63 *}

The penny drops. Sarah shakes her head in mock disbelief.

{SARAH: Some anthropologist.}
CHARLIE: She was having an affair?
SARAH: Of course she was having an affair.

SCENE 62   INT. THE OFFICE – THE POLICE STATION. NIGHT. {63 *}
The video screen shows Kate with the body. By now Sarah has opened her medical bag and is saying something to Kate. Ray can see himself clearing people away, including Gordon and the camera. Les hovers ineffectually but Kate is inconsolable. She is screaming something into the empty desert

3. If a scene from the shooting script was cut from the film it has no final film version scene number.

{SCENE 105 INT./ EXT. TOM'S FOUR-WHEEL-DRIVE –
THE SPINIFEX PLAIN. DAY .

The engine roars as Ray urges his vehicle on.}

4. Braces around text, whether dialogue or a scene description, indicate it was not included in the finished film.

Simon Lyndon as Ricko. Photo: Elise Lockwood.

MAIN CAST [in order of appearance]

JARED	Laurence Breuls
DIANE	Linda Cropper
RICKO	Simon Lyndon
RACHEL	Jessica Napier
TRACY	Boyana Novakovic
DET. SGT. WILANSKY	Chris Haywood
DET. GILHOOLEY	Essie Davis
CHERIE	Rebecca Smart
TIFFANY	Justine Clarke
LESLEY WARNER	Jeanette Cronin
KEN WARNER	David Field
GLENYS	Shayne Francis
TOBY	Heath Ledger
STEWART ACKLAND	Geoff Morell
LEN KIRBY	John Howard
GEOFF	John O'Hare
DOCTOR	Kate Sheil
DAVO	Brendan Donoghue
JASON	Cameron Nugent
SCOTT	Jade Gatt
KEMEL	George Basha
LEANNE	Nichole Avramidis
SHANA	Leeanna Walsman
LEESHA	Kellie Bright

Produced by David Elfick
Directed by Steve Vidler
Written by Nick Enright

Complete film credits appear at the end of the book.

PRINCIPAL CHARACTERS

JARED KIRBY, 17
DIANE, his mother
BRETT RICKETSON [RICKO], 22

SCHOOL
RACHEL ACKLAND, 16
CHERIE MILENKO, 15
TRACY WARNER, 15
LEANNE, 16
SHANA, 16
CRAIG DAVIDSON [DAVO], 17
KEMEL AYOUB, 17
SCOTT BLAYLOCK [SCOTTIE], 15
JASON, 17

BLACKROCK
KEN & LESLEY WARNER, Tracy's parents
GLENYS, Cherie's mother
GEOFF
TIFFANY, 21

ACROSS THE RIVER
LEN KIRBY, Jared's father
DET. SGT. WILANSKY
DET. GILHOOLEY
STEWART ACKLAND, Rachel's father
TOBY ACKLAND, Rachel's brother

SCENE 1 EXT. ON THE WATER – BLACKROCK BEACH. EARLY MORNING.

Cloudless sky meets endless ocean. Surfers sit on the swell. A wave comes. The boards turn in unison and the young riders seize their moment. One boy paddles out, busting through a wave: Jared, seventeen, strong body, sensitive features. He turns his board and looks back to shore …Beyond the beach is no glimpse of paradise but the grunge and grind of an industrial city. Chimneys belch smoke into the morning sky. Jared rides in. He cuts back deftly into the wave, then drops back in to ride to shore.

{SCENE 2 EXT. THE SHORE-LINE – BLACKROCK BEACH. EARLY MORNING.

Jared passes Cherie, a scrawny fifteen-year-old with a boogie board. She cheers as, on the water, Tracy, a lithe blonde teenage girl, stands up on her board.

CHERIE: Hey, Jared? Show us how you drop in after that cutback.

> *Jared flashes a look: as if. Tracy loses balance, tumbling in the shallows. Jared hoots.*

JARED: Can't teach something like that. You got to have the instinct.
CHERIE: Frogshit! Ricko taught you. Come on …

> *The surfers head up the beach.*

JARED: We got to get to school, Cherie.
CHERIE: Some other time. Any time. When?
JARED: Come down Sunday morning, early.

> *He hurries after his mates and falls into step with them.}*

SCENE 3 EXT. THE BEACHFRONT – BLACKROCK BEACH. EARLY MORNING.

Jared, wiry Davo, muscle-bound Jason – all seventeen – and Scottie, a baby-faced fifteen-year-old grommet, are under outdoor showers. Schoolbags and gear are on the concrete nearby. Scottie sees Cherie and Tracy coming up the beach. He flashes at the girls. Jason snaffles Scottie's undies, towel and bag, and sprints off with his board. Scottie howls. Davo and Jared follow Jason, pissing themselves, leaving Scottie naked under the water. He runs after them. They scatter his clothes along the road. The girls gleefully point to his bare behind, white between his tan-lines.

CHERIE: Baby's bum!

He gives them the finger before sprinting for his towel.

SCENE 4 INT. A DOCTOR'S SURGERY. DAY.   {7}

Diane, thirty-nine, lies on a table, shoulders bare, the tops of her breasts visible. A gloved hand holding a biopsy needle descends on her left breast. A doctor murmurs soothing words. She's apprehensive as the needle enters. Her face is strong, intelligent, weathered, watchful.

{SCENE 5 INT./EXT. THE VERANDAH – A NURSING HOME. DAY.

Diane hurries past elderly residents towards ...}

SCENE 6 INT. THE KITCHEN AND HALL – THE NURSING HOME. DAY.   {8}

Diane buttons her smock as Lesley Warner, petite, thirty-five, fills teapots from an urn.

LESLEY: How did you get on?

Diane looks up sharply.

At the dentist?

Reminded of her fib, Diane gives the thumbs-up as they steer the tea-trolleys into a hallway, towards the old folks.

SCENE 7 EXT. THE HIGH SCHOOL – TOWN. AFTERNOON.   {3}

An empty playground. Through windows, glimpses of classes in progress. A bell signals a rush to the gates and freedom.

SCENE 8 EXT. – THE FRONT GATES - THE HIGH SCHOOL AFTERNOON. {4}

Jared waits with his bag. His Blacko mates join him, led by Jason, Davo and stocky Lebanese Kemel, seventeen. Young Scottie runs after them. Rachel approaches. The Blackos exchange sardonic looks and head off. Davo and Jason tap Jared's fist in the ultra-cool surfie version of 'giving five'.

Rachel is sixteen, slim, dark, well-groomed, with skin that hasn't seen much sun; not an obvious partner for Jared. As he goes to kiss her, the Blacko girls, Cherie, Leanne and Shana pass them, staring. Over Rachel's shoulder, Jared threatens them. Rachel turns to discover the trio of disdainful younger girls. She leads Jared out of the yard. He puts an arm round her. Behind them, Shana mimics him, putting her arm over Leanne's shoulder.

SCENE 9 INT. THE FOYER – ACKLAND ADVERTISING AGENCY. DAY. {5}

Perfect male and female bodies in underwear, on posters bearing a post-modern brand-name in funky type – 'Body Count' –, line a state-of-the-art foyer, where strikingly beautiful models of both sexes sit with portfolios. Jared is awestruck. Rachel waves to the stylish receptionist, leads him to the inner sanctum. Jared turns back for a last look at the models ... colliding with a secretary. A cool, elegant model, Leesha, suppresses a laugh.

{SCENE 10 INT. THE DARK ROOM – ACKLAND ADVERTISING AGENCY. DAY

Blow-ups dry under infra-red light. Rachel works. Jared hangs another picture up.

JARED: This place is so cool.

As she passes, he nuzzles into her neck.

RACHEL: You got the horn? For me or those models?
JARED: Just for you ... Claudia.

She hits him. They kiss deeply. On the line a stark image has emerged: in front of a Lebanese takeaway Kemel, a stocky boy, shows his strength by shouldering Scottie. Cherie stares, unimpressed. Tracy's pretty young face looks straight to camera.}

SCENE 11 INT. THE ART DEPARTMENT – ACKLAND ADVERTISING AGENCY. DAY. {6}

A little later. Jared's photos lie scattered on the floor as Rachel and Jared sort through refuse, improvising a collage.

JARED: Shit! People get paid to work here. I'd do it for nothing.

Rachel puts stuff into a Gladbag. Jared sifts through Body Count offcuts: slices and shards of beautiful bodies.

STEWART: [*out of view*] Hey!

Stewart Ackland appears in the doorway, groomed, fit, forty-two, in shirt-sleeves. Behind him, a model passes on her way out.

What are you knocking off?

Stewart comes in, and surveys the mess on the floor.

RACHEL: It's creative recycling. This is Jared.
JARED: Mr Ackland...

Stewart shakes his hand.

STEWART: Stewart. You're the photographer?
JARED: Wannabe.

Stewart sees the splay of newly developed pictures: surf, steelworks, beach, skateboard heroics...

STEWART: These yours?

Jared nods diffidently. Stewart surveys them, impressed. He hands them back as Leesha looms in the corridor.

RACHEL: When are you shooting this one?
STEWART: Saturday night.

Leesha hovers.

RACHEL: Can we come?

Jared's eyes light up.

JARED: We could be slave labour.
STEWART: Okay. Now get out of here.
{JARED: Cool. Thanks.

Rachel heads off with a bulging Gladbag. Jared is stopped by Stewart's hand on his shoulder.

STEWART: Jared … are you sleeping with her?
JARED: Not yet. I'd like to be …

He meets Stewart's level gaze.

She could do heaps worse, eh?

Stewart is amused.}

{SCENE 12 EXT. A FOOTBRIDGE OVER THE RAILWAY LINE – TOWN. DAY

Two figures in school uniform, carrying garbage bags, cross a railway bridge towards a small wharf on a wide busy river …

SCENE 13 EXT. THE TOWN WHARF. DAY.

Rachel and Jared reach the bottom of the spiral staircase descending from the bridge. They kiss. He hears a sucking sound. Davo, Kemel and Jason, trailed by Scottie, head towards them. Davo sniffs his finger, licks it. The others snigger. Jared hoiks a stone. Davo and Jared scuffle.

JARED: Just 'cause you only know slags, Davo …

He cuffs Davo, who runs off laughing. The wharf fills rapidly with commuters and amateur fishermen. A ferry docks, letting off passengers. Cherie passes with Shana and Leanne. They check out Rachel with cool hostility. Jared kisses Rachel, more swiftly than before.

See ya.
RACHEL: I want to ride over with you.

Jared shakes his head, aware of the watching girls.

Okay, then I'll wave goodbye …

She pulls out her hankie and starts to wave. He grins, leads the way to the ferry.}

SCENE 14 EXT. A BRIDGE TO BLACKROCK. DAY.   {10}

A concrete and steel span straddles river and docks. Beyond it, the dark and massive silhouette of the steelworks against the afternoon sky. A battered and dust-encrusted red panel van rides the curve of the bridge like a wave.

SCENE 15 INT./EXT. THE FERRY. DAY.   {9}

Kemel, Jason and Davo {play a portable computer game. They} see Rachel get on with Jared.

KEMEL: Hey, Rachel! Coming over to check out the real men?

> *He and Jason flex their muscles jokingly. She ignores them. The couple sit on their own. A deck-hand pulls the gangplank up. The mooring-rope is loosened. Cherie looks out: Tracy is running down the ramp.*

CHERIE: Wait!

> *The deck-hand ignores her. Tracy leaps as the ferry pulls away, balancing outside the rail before vaulting it to land beside her mates. Cherie and the other kids cheer.*

DECK-HAND: That's against the law.

> *Tracy blows him a kiss. She sits with her gang as the little boat pulls away from the city-side dock.*

SCENE 16 EXT. THE MAIN STREET – BLACKROCK. DAY. {11}

The red van rounds a corner and bounces past a garage, fast-food joints, screeching to a halt at a red light near a bakery where Tiffany, twenty-one, dyed blonde, a bit lived-in, is behind the counter in a smock. She sees the van, runs into the street. Inside, a customer bangs on the window. The lights change. The van speeds off. Tiffany ignores the summons from inside, takes off her apron and follows the van.

SCENE 17 EXT. THE ROAD TO BLACKROCK WHARF. DAY.{12}

The red van careers down the road. Two twenty-ish surfers on foot recognise the driver, and yell, waving excitedly …

SURFERS: Ricko!

SCENE 18 INT./EXT. THE FERRY. DAY. {13}

Through the window, Blackrock wharf looms closer. Beyond the shed the red van throws some wild doughnuts around the turning circle. Dust and gravel fly. Jared rises in delighted surprise.

SCOTTIE: Shit, it's Ricko!
JASON: Hey, Ricko!

The other Blackos all stir, following Jared's gaze. Suddenly the boys whistle and yell. Cherie and the girls rush to the near side of the boat, looking out to the wharf. Rachel rises, slips her bag over her shoulders, joins Jared. He looks somewhat shamefaced.

Look … I'll catch you tomorrow. Okay?
RACHEL: Oh … Okay.

Disappointed, she watches him disembark with the Blackos.

SCENE 19 EXT. BLACKROCK WHARF. DAY. {14}

Leaning against the van, smoking, is Ricko, blond, twenty-two, with a surfer's body, a wicked grin and a good-looking face that has seen some hard living. The boys surge round him. He slaps Scottie round the head, pummels Jared.

JASON: You're back, Ricko!
RICKO: No, this is a hologram, Jason, you tonk.

Jared and Ricko pile in the van and drive off, scattering the other Blacko guys with the blast of a hoon-horn. Tiffany arrives, breathless, only to see them drive away.

SCENE 20 EXT. THE RICKETSON HOUSE – BLACKROCK. DAY. {15}

Jared sits in the van in the driveway of this shabby fibro cottage. Two bags of gear are thrust through an open window, followed by Ricko. He throws the gear and two big surfing trophies into the back of the van as his father, a wasted forty-five, lurches out into the front yard and runs towards the van. Ricko leaps into the back and slams the doors.

RICKO: Go, mate! Go!

Jared slides into the driver's seat and takes off. The van screeches away. Ricko's father runs alongside, punching at the window.

SCENE 21   INT./EXT. RICKO'S VAN – BLACKROCK. DAY. {16}

The two guys are convulsed. Ricko climbs into the front. Jared {sees a snake tattoo on Ricko's biceps. He pokes it, chortles, and} pulls up at a red light. A figure darts from behind the van to the driver's window. A fist connects with Jared, startling him. At the end of the fist is Tiffany, breathless.

JARED: Shit, Tiffany!

> *She sees it's him.*

TIFFANY: Sorry, Jared.

> *She runs round to the passenger window and punches Ricko.*

You bastard, Ricko! Not a fuckin' word in eleven months.

> *He laughs as she lays into him, then kisses him passionately.*

Come on, tell me you missed me, you bastard.
RICKO: I missed you, you bastard.

> *Jared hoots. Tiffany hits him again.*

No, Tiff! I missed you heaps.

> *She goes to get in the van.*

We'll catch you later, up the rock. Jazza and me are on a mission.

> *Jared drives off at speed, sounding his horn.*

SCENE 22   EXT. BLACKROCK WHARF. DUSK.   {17}

As the lights go on over town commuters get off the ferry. Lesley and Diane are among them.

SCENE 23   EXT. THE KIRBY HOUSE – THE STREET. DUSK.{18}

Lesley and Diane cross the street carrying groceries. Two grommets on bikes make raucous horn sounds as they flash past the women, nearly knocking Lesley over. Diane steadies her.

DIANE: Aren't you glad you got daughters?
LESLEY: Sometimes …

Linda Cropper as Diane. Photo: Elise Lockwood.

They approach Diane's gate. Surfie thrash sounds inside.

DIANE: Swap you any time.

Lesley heads down the street. Diane opens the door …

SCENE 24 INT. THE LIVING-ROOM – THE KIRBY HOUSE. DUSK.   {19}

… And nearly trips over a pile of Ricko's gear. As she stares at the two big surfing trophies, a naked athletic male body, dripping wet, yelling, bounds into the hall, colliding with her. She jumps.

RICKO: Shit, mate, I fuckin' scalded myself!

He sees her, grins. Jared appears from the living room, finds the pair face to face in the midst of the gear.

Been that long since I saw hot running water.
DIANE: Hello, Brett.

He waves affably, returns to the bathroom.

SCENE 25 INT. THE KITCHEN – THE KIRBY HOUSE. DUSK.{20}

Diane unpacks the groceries in silence.

JARED: It'd just be till he gets settled.
DIANE: He's not staying here, Jared.
JARED: I've already asked him.
DIANE: Then unask him.
JARED: Mum! His old man doesn't want to know.
DIANE: Neither do I, mate. I got worries of my own.
JARED: What? Like pulling a guy? If you nag them the way you nag me …

He stops dead. They both know he's gone too far.

Sorry. That was off.

Ricko's there, in jeans. He slicks back his wet hair, grins.

RICKO: No sweat. I'll be okay in the van.

Jared storms out of the room. Diane stops Ricko.

DIANE: Nothing against you, Brett. Just … they're working them hard
  at school.
{RICKO: Holidays coming up, but. Eh?
DIANE: And then Year Twelve.}

SCENE 26 INT. THE FRONT DOOR – THE KIRBY HOUSE. DUSK. {21}

Jared is at the van outside, loading up Ricko's gear. Diane holds the door open for Ricko.

RICKO: You're all right, Diane. Pull a guy any time, I reckon.

  He winks. She smiles wryly.

DIANE: Thanks, Brett.

  He's gone. She turns off the music. She finds the trophies which the boys have left behind.

SCENE 27 INT. A TATTOO PARLOUR. NIGHT. {24}

Jared has a tattoo pricked onto his biceps. Ricko's biceps is bared. The tattooist copies his tattoo: a fish skeleton.

SCENE 28 EXT. THE HEADLAND – BLACKROCK. NIGHT.{22}

A 'session': the older surfers from the road, Davo and Jason and other younger guys share a smoke round Ricko. Tiffany leans on him. Scottie hangs on the outer edge, listening.

{RICKO: Waves … Like youse never seen. Kangaroo Island, going off!
  Streaky Bay. All the way up to Flat Rocks. Eight thousand Ks
  there and back. The last fuckin' frontier.

  Still agitated, Jared stares down at the water. Ricko eases Tiffany aside and rolls towards Jared, passing the joint.}

(Note: *in the finished film an improvisation was used for this scene with several changes in the dialogue. The major change was Ricko's first speech:*

RICKO: One hell day while I'm just sitting out the back see these other dudes just paddling for the horizon, the whole thing just picked up like a slut, no mucking around. Well I just start fucking paddling for my life, the lip starts feathering, just about at the top ... prick fucking launched me down to the bottom straight under ... no fucking 'round ... I thought I was going to get locked in a cave, eh.

They all laugh–Ricko has a bong.

Whose is this shit? Is this your shit? It's a fucking flame thrower this thing. Here, suck on this one brother.

To Jared.)

Get over it, mate. I'm over it, eh?
JARED: Yeah. Hey ... glad you're back.
RICKO: What are you, a queer dog?
JARED: Get fucked.
RICKO: Suss dog.

Ricko lies back, draws on the joint. Tiffany opens a bag.

TIFFANY: Want a doughnut? They're only yesterday's.

Jared takes one, munches. He looks down to the beach. A light burns over the surf-club. A caretaker is locking up. Suddenly Jared stands and calls down to him ...

JARED: Hey, Charlie ...

The caretaker stops, looks towards the rock. Jared takes off down the rocky slope.

RICKO: Where you going, mate?

Jared stops halfway downhill to the beach.

JARED: Get the club house Saturday night ...

Ricko, Tiffany and the guys look down at him.

We'll put on a keg for you, mate. The rave from hell.

He reaches the caretaker in the carpark.

RICKO: That's my man. How come you never thought of it, Tiff?

TIFFANY: I don't like you that much.

(Note: In the finished film the improvised scene continues:

> RICKO: Fuck you.

> *They kiss. The boys whoop.*

> TIFFANY: Oh shut up, right.

> *Ricko laughs.)*

{SCENE 29   THE ART ROOM – THE HIGH SCHOOL. DAY.

Students and a female teacher prepare an exhibition. Jared is up a ladder. He makes a jagged collage of body parts from the raid on the agency. Rachel fixes hessian to a frame. Amid the collage Jared places his own grunge shots.

RACHEL: How come I've never seen him round?
JARED: He headed off just after Christmas. Following the waves sort of thing …

> *The teacher passes, pauses near a student's work: a tight-arsed display of still-life studies. She addresses the room.*

TEACHER: I don't want correct. I don't want nice. I want your world. Your statement …

> *On the body parts Jared tries a photo of the Blackos on the concrete beachfront … then Scottie executing a smart skateboard manoeuvre, caught in mid-flight.*

JARED: When I was, like, eleven, I came off my skateboard down the half-pipe. Ricko found me with my head split open, grabbed some guy's keys, drove me to casualty, got me stitched, called Mum, brought me home. And he'd never even driven before, only watched. That's Ricko. Total legend. They'll all turn out for Ricko.

> *He steps back from the work. Rachel stands close to him.*

How's this?
RACHEL: It's a statement.

SCENE 30 EXT. THE FRONT GATES – THE HIGH SCHOOL. AFTERNOON.

Jared collects money from town guys.

TOWN GUY: Five bucks!

> *Davo, Kemel, Jason and the Blacko boys pass in a clump.*

JASON: If youse don't pay, youse don't front.

> *The town guys pay Jared and head off as Rachel approaches.*

RACHEL: You want to come home for a while?
JARED: I better get home. Have to pay for the club house.

> *He counts and sorts the money. Cherie, Tracy and Shana pass. Cherie holds out five dollars. He snorts.*

JARED: In your dreams, Cherie.

> *She squares up to him. He swings his bag at her. The girls snigger and run away down the hill. The yard is empty. He kisses Rachel quickly.*

JARED: Hey, Saturday night …

> *She looks into his eyes. He's suddenly nervous, expectant.*

RACHEL: Yeah. About time, eh?

> *He nods, then kisses her. The art teacher passes, smiles at them. Embarrassed, Jared heads down the hill.*}

SCENE 31 INT. THE DOCTOR'S SURGERY. DAY   {23}

Diane gazes steadily across a desk. Her arms are folded protectively across her body.

{DOCTOR: You may need time to think this through, talk about it with your family …}
DIANE: If it's the only option …

> {S*he looks out the window. A seagull lands on the ledge, then flies off into blue sky.*}

DOCTOR: The hospital will call as soon as a bed comes free. I'll put you in touch with our support service …

Diane grimaces. The doctor smiles reassurance.

DOCTOR: Women who've been through the same experience …
DIANE: It's an experience, is it? …
DOCTOR: And remember, there's always the possibility of a reconstruction …

SCENE 32 INT. THE BATHROOM – THE KIRBY HOUSE. EARLY EVENING. {25}

Diane soaps herself under the shower, enjoying the stream of water. She reaches her breasts, weighing them in her hands. She senses another presence beyond the shower curtain … Jared in a towel, shaving at the mirror, wiping it to clear the steam. She reaches for a towel.

DIANE: Don't knock or anything.
JARED: Nothing I haven't seen.

He goes on shaving. She glimpses the tattoo on his biceps.

DIANE: That had better be a transfer.

She reaches to touch it. He pulls his arm away.

Just don't get one that says 'Mum'.
JARED: No way.
DIANE: You still cranky with me?

He steps under the shower and slings his towel over the rail. She wipes the mirror and looks at herself.

You in for tea? Be nice to sit down to a meal together.
JARED: I got Ricko's rave, Mum!

He looks round the curtain. He sees her disappointment.

What?
DIANE: Few things I want to talk over.

He frowns and ducks back under the water.

Not everything's about you, mate. I've got some stuff happening.
JARED: Tomorrow, okay?

His voice is muffled by the shower. She watches her face disappear as the mirror mists again.

SCENE 33 EXT. THE SPORTS OVAL – BLACKROCK. EARLY EVENING.   {26}

Under a single shaft of light behind the bleachers, Shana and Leanne help Cherie into a skimpy dress. Tracy supplies earrings and lipstick. Cherie giggles. They hide her T-shirt and shorts under the stand. They check her out. Clutching a bottle of Kahlua, Shana leads them into the night.

SCENE 34 EXT. AN OLD FACTORY SITE. EARLY EVENING. {27}

Beautiful female models in underwear stand against the brick and rusted iron of a loading bay. Nearby is a muscular male model in shorts, singlet and workboots. All is elegant, cool, ready for a Bruce Weber to shoot a starkly sensual black-and-white spread. Rachel and Toby watch Stewart shooting. Toby gazes at the models, rapt. Stewart is happy with the shot. Wardrobe bring coats.

STEWART: Great. Let's have … this one …

> *He indicates an angular blonde, Leesha.*

RACHEL: They do have names.
LEESHA: Leesha.
STEWART: Leesha … up there.

> *He points up. A winch hangs over an open upper storey door. It's a sheer drop to the concrete below.*

LEESHA: You're joking.
STEWART: This will be a high-profile campaign. With you or with someone else, Leesha.

> *There's no threat apparent in his tone. She throws him her coat and strides towards the building. He and his assistant see her body entering the field of white light.*

ASSISTANT: You wouldn't get me up there.
STEWART: Mate, I wouldn't want you up there.

> *Leesha appears at the high open doorway. The assistant angles a light up on her. She looks eerily beautiful. Stewart is right: it will be brilliant, a killer shot. He turns in irritation as a vehicle approaches. Ricko's van pulls up, breaking the mood of quiet concentration. Jared piles out. He's dressed down in black T-shirt and ripped black jeans. Stewart sees him, mutters to Rachel …*

Late.

... Then looks past him to Ricko, also in black, with Tiffany, who's having a bad hair day ... Kemel, Davo and young Scottie, and three or four more older Blacko surfers ... all piling out of the back of the van. Stewart glimpses a mattress, pillows, slabs of stubbies.. The guys wave to Toby, who acknowledges them. Then they see the models, the shoot in progress. They gaze open-mouthed.

JARED: Hi, Mr Ackland. Uh ... Rachel ... Rachel, this is Ricko.

Ricko sees Stewart staring at him, grins, points to the models.

RICKO: Shit, mate, it's a hard life.

Jared feels Stewart's disapproval.

JARED: Better get going, eh?
STEWART: I thought you were here to work?

Jared awkwardly indicates the vanload of Blackos.

JARED: Got a bit of a party on over home.

He goes. Rachel starts to follow him and the group.

STEWART: Rachel!

Jared sees him take her aside out of earshot, beckoning Toby to join the family huddle. Jared waits anxiously. Tiffany, Scottie, Kemel and Davo and the surfers stare at the shoot. Toby leaves his father and sister. Stewart's voice is suddenly raised.

STEWART: Toby's eighteen, that's the difference.
RACHEL: Toby's got a dick, that's the difference!

The argument continues. Jared sees Toby get into the Volvo. He drives past the Blackos. Jared stands in front of the van.

TOBY: See you over there, dudes ...

He speeds away. Stewart gets ready to shoot.

RACHEL: He won't let me.
JARED: Shit!
RACHEL: Stay and watch for a while?

Ricko turns the engine on, catching Jared in the headlights. Their beam lights the models, ruining the shot. Stewart irritably waves the van away. Ricko nudges the van forward, bumping Jared.

**{SCENE 35   INT./ EXT. RICKO'S VAN – THE OLD FACTORY
SITE. EARLY EVENING.}**

*(Note: in the finished film this scene is continuous with the previous.) Jared piles
into the back with Kemel, Davo and Scottie. {The van is lined with mementos of
Ricko's surf odyssey.} Ricko takes off at speed. Jared looks out the back window
to see Leesha positioned on her dangerous, stylish perch.*

SCENE 36   EXT. THE ROAD TO BLACKROCK BEACH.
NIGHT.   {28}

*{Gary's music is on the air.}   Shana, Cherie, Leanne and Tracy head for the
party. {Shana leads, humming: 'Do To Me What Your Eyes Say You Want To
Do'. The others bop along behind her. Tracy has a little tinkling bell round her
neck.} A Volvo passes them, slows down. The driver is Toby, alone.*

TRACY: Hi, Toby.

> *The other girls giggle, embarrassing her.*

TOBY: Want a ride?
CHERIE: We're nearly there.

> *But Shana opens the back door and gets in. Leanne follows, leaving Tracy
> and Cherie on the side of the road.*

TOBY: One of you can get in the front.

> *Cherie shoves Tracy into the front seat, and joins the other two in the back,
> giggling. Tracy's bell tinkles …*

SCENE 37   EXT. THE SURF CLUB – BLACKROCK BEACH.
NIGHT.   {29}

*Kids see the van approach with a figure straddling its bonnet: Ricko, riding the van
like a chariot. It pulls up. Toby and the girls arrive. The girls are craning out the
windows staring as Ricko grins, acknowledging applause as he jumps off: the legend
returned. Jason collects bets from the guys.*

JARED: Eh, Toby. Give it a go?

Left to right: Justine Clarke as Tiffany, Boyana Novakovic as Tracy, Nichole Avramidis as Leanne and Rebecca Smart as Cherie. Photo: Elise Lockwood.

Toby looks askance: as if. He locks the Volvo, moves towards the club, then realises that the girls aren't following but watching Jared strap himself to the roof of the van. It takes off, with Jared riding and whooping like Ben Hur on speed.

SCENE 38 INT. DIANE'S ROOM – THE KIRBY HOUSE. NIGHT. {30}

Diane folds a night-dress into an overnight bag, closes it.

SCENE 39 INT. THE MOSH PIT – THE SURF CLUB. NIGHT. {31}

Gary, thin, pale and skinny with a quiff of purple hair, plays lead guitar with his grunge band. Davo leaps up onto the stage. The crowd shouts …

KIDS: Dav-o! Dav-o!

He dives into the crowd to surf the pit. Scottie apes Davo. Kemel makes the crowd part. Scottie falls splat on the floor. Jared and Ricko whistle, clap. The party has kicked in. Jared has made it happen. Ricko slaps him around the head happily, as around them sixty or more kids and older surfers get into it. Jared has his camera, and starts shooting:

*Shana and the girls are in band-moll mode (*snap*) as Gary turns it on (*snap*). Shana reaches up to grope him (*snap*). He's cool: this is a rock star's life (*snap*). Shana dances with Leanne (*snap*). Tracy drinks with Cherie (*snap*). Tracy rings her bell for Jared (*snap*) …*

Jared takes a break as Ricko gives him a stubbie. He sees Jason move in on Leanne. Shana, Cherie and Tracy approach Ricko and Jared boldly, giggling, watched by Toby.

SHANA: Check this, Ricko …

She tinkles Tracy's bell. Tracy slaps her hand.

You know why she wears it? So when it rings, you know she's coming …

Tracy is embarrassed but convulsed. The girls run away, laughing. Tracy starts dancing as she goes, losing Cherie and Shana in the crush on the floor. She checks out Toby. Jared watches Tracy. Ricko watches Jared.

RICKO: Mate, go for it.

Jared flushes, sprung. Ricko chuckles.

JARED: Mate, me and Rachel are … you know.

RICKO: But Daddy wouldn't let her front. She won't know nothing. Eh?

Jared shakes his head. Ricko gestures with his bottle-neck towards Tracy. He watches Jared move towards her. They start dancing. Jared slings his camera over his back to get closer.

SCENE 40 EXT. BLACKROCK WHARF. NIGHT.   {32}

(Note: in the finished film this scene is intercut with the final image of the previous.) The river is silent, dark but for a lantern of light across the water, as the ferry glides towards the jetty. There's a single passenger inside: Rachel.

SCENE 41 INT. THE FRONT HALL AND FAMILY ROOM – THE MILENKO HOUSE. NIGHT.   {33}

Diane pushes past an open screen door, walks down the hall.

DIANE: It's me, Glenys.

She reaches the family room at the back of the house. Glenys, casual, attractive, late thirties, sits watching TV.

GLENYS: If I'd known you were home on your own …

DIANE: Kevin Costner stood me up, darl.

She sits beside Glenys, moving the videotape box. She glances at the title: Terms of Endearment.

GLENYS: Did you bring your Kleenex?

Glenys passes Diane a joint. Diane declines, watching the screen: Debra Winger battles cancer. Shirley MacLaine rages.

DIANE: Christ, it's Saturday night, Glenny! We need a few laughs!

She turns off the video. Glenys groans in protest.

GLENYS: Diane!

DIANE: You know how it ends. She carks it, all right? Like they always do, looking fabulous to the end. Come on.

She drags Glenys out the door.

SCENE 42 INT. THE MOSH PIT – THE SURF CLUB. NIGHT.{34}

Music. Jared dances closer to Tracy. He plays with her bell. Toby, pissed, looms on them.

TOBY: Hey, Kirby! You're meant to be going with my sister.
JARED: Shit, we're only dancing.
RICKO: Free country, Nigel.
TOBY: Toby! Tracy came with me.
JARED: Don't be a dickhead, Ackland. She came with Cherie and them.

Toby shoves him. Tracy watches, bewildered. Jared shoves back. The boys square up to one another.

TOBY: Back off, you fuckin' hoon!
JARED: You want a smack in the head? Don't call me a hoon, fuckin' townie wanker …

He smacks Toby round the head. Toby retaliates. Swiftly, Ricko joins them, grabbing Toby hard by the throat.

TOBY: Shit, Kirby. Thought we were mates.

Jared eases Ricko off Toby. Tracy comforts Toby.

TRACY: Never had anyone fighting over me.

Jared strides out. Ricko follows …

SCENE 43 EXT. THE SURF CLUB – BLACKROCK BEACH. NIGHT.   {35}

RICKO: Where you going, mate?

Jared doesn't answer, heads for the beach. Under a lamp-post Cherie pashes Scottie. Near his van, Gary swigs Jack Daniels with his band mates. Shana slides away from the guys and reaches Tracy, who is drinking Kahlua. Shana looks towards the road.

SHANA: Shit, the rich bitch.

Rachel approaches out of the darkness.

RACHEL: Hi. Have you seen Jared?
SHANA: Seen him? We've had him, haven't we, Trace?

Tracy giggles, nods.

Get over it. Heaps of other guys out there. Anywhere out there …

She offers Rachel a drink. Rachel pushes the bottle away and hurries off. The girls laugh helplessly.

SCENE 44 EXT. BLACKROCK BEACH. NIGHT. {36}

The soft roll of the ocean soothes Jared. The moon shines on the water. He strips off, lays his camera carefully on his T-shirt, and dives in, enjoying the gentle waves.

SCENE 45 EXT. THE SURF CLUB – BLACKROCK BEACH. NIGHT. {38}

Rachel stands in the doorway, looking. Gary and the band are back on stage. She is startled by a wild scream as, chased by Jason, Leanne runs {under the lamp post} towards Cherie and Shana.

LEANNE: Jason showed me his dick! It's got a flappy bit on the end.
JASON: Shit, Leanne! Now they'll all want a look …

Jason chases her off. Davo whispers a horny secret to Scottie and Kemel. They chortle. Rachel approaches them.

RACHEL: Guys? You seen Jared?

They ignore her. Scottie and Kemel hare off after Davo.

CHERIE: Scottie! Wait …

{Rachel approaches Cherie who watches the disappearing boys.

CHERIE: Dickheads …
RACHEL: You seen Jared?
CHERIE: He went off down the beach.

Rachel heads towards the beach.}

Boyana Novakovic as Tracy. Photo: Elise Lockwood.

SCENE 46   EXT. BLACKROCK BEACH. NIGHT.   {39}

Jared emerges from the water. He dries himself on his T-shirt, pulls his jeans on. He starts to climb the headland.

SCENE 47 INT. THE GAMING ROOM – THE WORKERS' CLUB. NIGHT.   {40}

Glenys watches as Diane, drink in hand, feeds a poker-machine. She loses ... loses again ... suddenly a cascade of coins tumbles out. She whoops. Two fortyish blokes, Geoff and Stan, move in on them. Diane gathers the money. Geoff applauds. Diane nudges Glenys.

DIANE: Reckon he's after a free drink?
GEOFF: I'm after a small loan.

    Diane and Glenys chuckle. The men introduce themselves.

SCENE 48 EXT. THE HEADLAND – BLACKROCK. NIGHT.{41}

Jared smokes, alone with the sea and sky. Below him, the beach is in shadow. Suddenly, disconnected sounds, movement across the sand. A boy draws a girl down the beach. She sounds excited and drunk. They sink to the ground, embracing clumsily. He rolls on top of her.

SCENE 49 INT. THE PARTY ROOM – THE WORKERS' CLUB. NIGHT.   {42}

Glenys, Diane and the blokes pass the doors of the party-room. A male stripper, a Fabio clone, is doing his stuff for a hens' night. The women check him out.

GEOFF: I could look like that if I had the time.
DIANE: Nobody's got that much time.

    The bride-to-be is urged on the stripper by her girlfriends. He grinds obligingly towards her. The WOMEN barrack. Shana's mum, thirty-five, happily drunk, waves to Glenys and Diane. She gestures to the stripper and the bride, rolls her eyes.

Beats a shower tea any day.

SHANA'S MOTHER: Jeez, I'm going to regret this tomorrow. Thanks for letting Shana sleep over.

Glenys is startled and suddenly alert.

GLENYS: Hang on! Cherie said she was staying at your place.

The other woman shakes her head. Light dawns on both.

Lying little bitch!

Diane sees her hurry out of the club. Geoff brings another drink for Diane, who decides to take it.

SCENE 50 EXT. THE HEADLAND – BLACKROCK. NIGHT.{43, 44}

(Note: in the finished film the following was treated as two scenes.) Jared looks down on the shadowed beach: the guy has his pants down. It's Toby. He and the girl are having sex. Whooping and calling, other guys reach the pair on the sand. Jared recognises Kemel and Davo, trailed by Scottie. The girl protests, struggling.

TOBY: [*faintly*] Don't kick me, bitch!

They seem to be holding her down. She cries out, 'Let me go!'

SCENE 51 EXT. THE TOILET BLOCK – BLACKROCK BEACH. NIGHT.   {37}

In the distance, Gary's band hits the peak of their set. Rachel stumbles through the shadows. Against the dunny-block wall she sees Ricko getting head from Tiffany. He meets Rachel's gaze, grins, then raises his eyebrows in invitation. She hurries off towards the water.

SCENE 52 EXT. THE HEADLAND – BLACKROCK. NIGHT.{47, 48}

(Note: in the finished film the following was treated as two scenes.) The moon emerges, lighting the beach and Jared, who stands staring down as the last of the rapists, Scottie, gets up, pulling his jeans up over the pale skin of his arse. Toby leads the boys up the beach, revealing a girl staggering to her feet, whimpering, 'Help me'. Around her neck a bell tinkles. Jared recognises Tracy, a small but distinct figure, standing helpless on the beach. On the night air, Gary's band hit the final chord of their last song. The crowd cheers and whistles. Jared is motionless. Then he starts to run ... and run ... away from the beach, from Tracy.

SCENE 53 INT. THE PARTY ROOM – THE WORKERS' CLUB. NIGHT. {45}

Music. The place still hops. Diane finishes her drink.

DIANE: I should hit the road ...
GEOFF: How about one last dance? First and last ... ?
DIANE: You don't look like a dancer.
GEOFF: You'd be surprised.

> *He moves closer. She finds she likes the idea. (Note: in the finished film this scene is followed by a short scene in the surf club in which Rachel searches through the raging party.)*

SCENE 54 EXT. THE REAR ENTRANCE – THE SURF CLUB. NIGHT. {49}

Silence. Gary and the band are bumping out their gear into the open van. Couples lie around, variously out of it or into it. Jason sits woozily, his arm round Leanne, who slumps, wasted, her head in her hands.

JASON: Look at them stars ... Beautiful, going on forever. Look, Leanne ...
LEANNE: Don't make me look up, Jason, I'll spew.

> *Cherie, also the worse for wear, approaches out of the darkness.*

CHERIE: You seen Scottie? Leanne?

> *No answer. She heads off.*

SCENE 55 EXT. NEAR THE HEADLAND – BLACKROCK BEACH. NIGHT. {50}

Rachel is anxious. The beach is silent in the moonlight.

RACHEL: Jared?

> *Ahead of her, in her path, something lies in the sand. Half-obscured by a rock is the lower half of an inert female form, one leg splayed out in Rachel's path.*

SCENE 56 EXT. THE SURF CLUB – BLACKROCK BEACH. NIGHT.   {51}

(Note: in the finished film this scene is intercut with the previous.) {*Kemel demolishes the last of the sausages.*} *Ricko, chest bare, hair wet, helps Scottie along, half-carrying the wasted kid. He sees Davo smoking.*

RICKO: Someone's got to get him home.
DAVO: Can't you, mate? You got the wheels.
RICKO: Well, open the doors!

> *Davo opens the van. Tiffany sprawls on the mattress, asleep.*

RICKO: I'm a fuckin' ambulance service.

> *Shana emerges from Gary's van. Gary lies behind her.*

SHANA: What time is it?

> *Cherie returns as Ricko and Jason lift Scottie into the van. He throws up again.*

JASON: Scottie, you fuckin' bogan!

> *An old car pulls up. Glenys gets out of it. She sees Cherie.*

GLENYS: You lying little hound!

> *The guys cheer and barrack as Glenys pursues Cherie round Gary's van, yelling her name. Suddenly Cherie freezes. Rachel stumbles towards them, stunned, oblivious of the chaos and cheering. Cherie's face reflects the distress she senses as Rachel feels a blur of faces, voices, shapes, swimming before her eyes.*

{SCENE 57 A STEEP ROAD – THE HILL. NIGHT.

Stewart, in his BMW, passes substantial houses, most in darkness. Outside one brightly lit house he sees two police cars. He pulls up …

SCENE 58 INT. THE LIVING ROOM – THE ACKLAND HOUSE. NIGHT.

… To find Marian in a dressing-gown with two officers, Toby dishevelled and drunk, and Rachel wrapped in a blanket. Her face is white, eyes wide.}

Above left to right: Simon Lyndon as Ricko, Justine Clarke as Tiffany, Shayne Francis as Glenys and Rebecca Smart as Cherie. Below: Rebecca Smart as Cherie. Photos: Elise Lockwood.

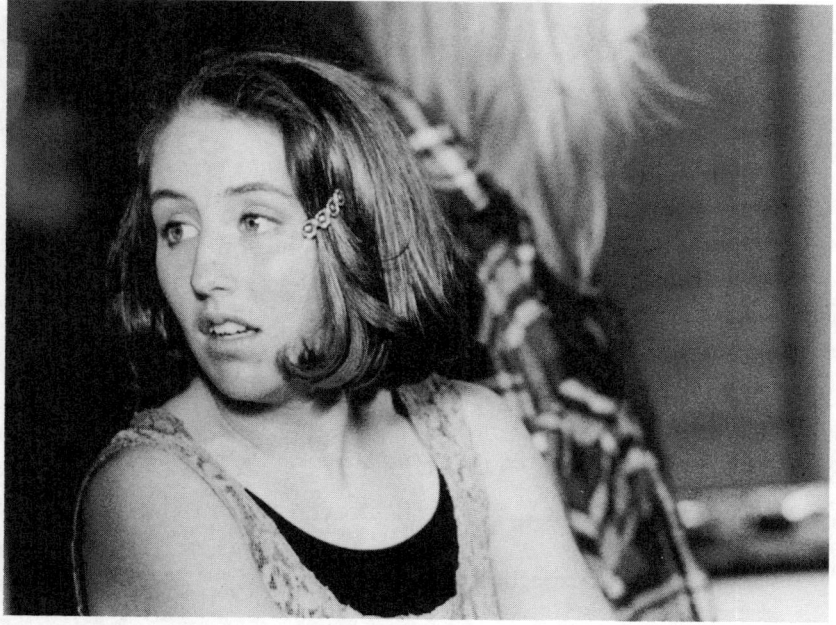

SCENE 59 INT. A SUBURBAN BEDROOM. PRE-DAWN.   {52}

Light peeps through the blinds. Diane stirs awake and discovers an unfamiliar room. She sees the sleeping man beside her: Geoff. She slides out of bed and stealthily starts dressing.

SCENE 60 EXT. NEAR THE HEADLAND – BLACKROCK BEACH. NIGHT.   {53}

Tracy staggers to her feet in shadow. She seems to look directly towards her watcher ...

TRACY: Help me.

> *The girl's image pulses and distorts. Someone is pounding ...*

SCENE 61 INT. JARED'S ROOM – THE KIRBY HOUSE. EARLY EVENING.   {54, 55}

... On the door. Jared stirs in his uneasy sleep, mutters a response. Diane comes in. His walls are lined with photos, stark and grungy. The only colour is a line of pictures of Rachel ... and, prominent as a shrine, an 'official' photo of Ricko winning a surf trophy, grinning at the camera. Flanking it are two real trophies.

DIANE: What time did you leave that party?

> *He's nonplussed.*

DIANE: Did you stay till the end?

> *He shakes his head. She sits on the bed.*

DIANE: I just heard down the shop. They found some kid dead on the beach.

> *He stares at her, clearing his throat.*

JARED: Who?

DIANE: A girl, I don't know who.

> *He turns away, buries his head in the pillow.*

DIANE: You're not that hung over! Do you hear me? Somebody's dead.

JARED: What do you expect me to do about it?

He burrows further into the pillow. There is a loud jarring noise overhead, as though over a battle zone. Diane draws the blind, letting in shafts of harsh sunlight. She looks up ... A TV news helicopter sweeps over Blackrock. (Note: in the finished film the helicopter is treated as a separate scene.)

SCENE 62 EXT. A STREET – BLACKROCK. MORNING. {56}

Kids speed on their bikes, trailing the chopper towards ... {57}

SCENE 63 EXT. BLACKROCK BEACH. MORNING. {58}

... A police search-party combing the sand with dogs. Some police lines have been set up. The club house is surrounded by official vehicles. News crews hurry towards the beach through the clumps of curious locals.

SCENE 64 EXT. THE MILENKO HOUSE – BLACKROCK. MORNING. {60}

Bright sunlight. Diane reaches the house as Glenys pursues Cherie out the front door.

GLENYS: You're grounded, you hear me?

> *Cherie pushes past Diane, her face screwed tight. Glenys winces as her bare feet hit the hot path.*

Cherie! You come back here! It could have been you, not Tracy! You hear me?

> *But the girl is halfway down the street.*

DIANE: 'Tracy'? Was it Tracy Warner? God, no ...

> *She hurries away down the street.*

SCENE 65 INT. CENTRAL POLICE STATION – THE CITY. DAY. . {59}

Photos of Tracy's body in situ are inspected by Detective Gilhooley, and her partner, Detective Sergeant Wilansky. He frowns at her squeamishness. She steels herself.

SCENE 66 EXT. THE WARNER HOUSE – THE STREET. DAY.{61}

Diane, passing the front fences of this working-class block, sees curious neighbours staring at Ken Warner at his front door, pushing away an insistent TV interviewer flanked by cameraman and sound recordist.

KEN: Just leave us alone!

Diane runs into the yard, grabs a garden hose and sprays the interviewer and his crew.

DIANE: Don't you understand plain English?

They retreat. She drops the hose.

INTERVIEWER: Are you a relative? Friend of the family?

She raises the hose again. They retreat further. She drops it. But they go on shooting.

INTERVIEWER: Is it true the party was unsupervised?

Diane attacks the camera with the stream of water, driving the crew off the property. Ken holds the screen door open as she mounts the front steps.

DIANE: It'll be me on the six o'clock news.

SCENE 67 INT. THE LIVING ROOM – THE WARNER HOUSE. DAY. {62}

A small girl, Tracy's sister, peers out from the kitchen doorway. An elderly female relative hovers.

DIANE: Bloody mongrels. Ken, I'm so sorry …

His face is closed against grief. She embraces him awkwardly. The phone rings. Ken turns to answer it.

SCENE 68 TRACY'S BEDROOM – THE WARNER HOUSE. DAY. {63}

Bright summer outside. The walls of the tiny room are lined with posters, photos, sports trophies and ribbons. Lesley stands at a corkboard pulling out pins, removing snapshots: Tracy at the beach; with the netball team; in a Pizza-Hut uniform. Diane puts an arm round her. She goes on working methodically, looking only at the board.

LESLEY: She told us they were having a sleepover at Shana's. I'd never think to check up. Why would she lie to us?

DIANE: Don't think about that, Lesley. She was a lovely girl, a good girl.

Lesley drops the pins in a dish.

LESLEY: That's not what they'll be saying out there.

She puts the photos away and starts taking down the ribbons. Ken comes in, propping himself up in the doorway.

KEN: That was the Pizza Hut wondering why she hadn't turned up for her shift ...

He puts his hand on a large jar of coins.

When they catch the animal that did that to her ...

DIANE: But it was an accident, wasn't it?

Ken looks up at her, unable to answer. Lesley shakes her head.

LESLEY: Ken had to go in and ...

Ken's control breaks. Lesley holds him tight as he's racked by sobs.

SCENE 69 EXT. THE KIRBY HOUSE – BLACKROCK. DAY. {64}

Jared {is ushered out of the house by a police officer. The woman next door, Mrs Lindsay, stares from her porch, as Jared} gets into the back seat of a waiting police car. It drives away as Diane turns into the street. The car passes her. Jared sees her. She glances in. Their eyes meet. He looks blank. The car pulls away, leaving her bewildered on the footpath.

{SCENE 70   INT. A SUBURBAN GARAGE. DAY.

Surrounded by gear, Gary and two band mates share a joint, listening to music on an old stained mattress. A door opens. A shaft of sun pierces the gloom. The boys squint. Gary's mother has someone behind her: a police officer.

SCENE 71 EXT. THE SPORTS OVAL – BLACKROCK. DAY.

Cherie, Shana and Leanne huddle round a boom-box, listening to a pop ballad, smoking, crying. They see a police car pull up beyond the outer fence. They rise slowly, staring at the approaching constable.

SCENE 72 INT./ EXT. AYOUB LEBANESE TAKEAWAY – BLACKROCK. AFTERNOON.

Kemel, serving in the shop, sees the cops pull up.

SCENE 73 EXT. ACROSS THE STREET FROM THE AYOUB LEBANESE TAKEAWAY – BLACKROCK. AFTERNOON.

Scottie hovers anxiously on a skateboard, watching Kemel get into the car. Then a policeman beckons to him.}

SCENE 74 INT. AN INTERVIEW ROOM – BLACKROCK POLICE STATION. DAY.   {65}

Jared sits opposite Detective Gilhooley, who writes onto a lap-top. Beyond a glass partition, other Blacko kids gather, waiting for their interviews. Detective Wilansky paces with coffee.

GILHOOLEY: That's all?
JARED: All I can remember.
WILANSKY: It was your party.
JARED: That's all the people I knew.

> *He starts to get up.*

GILHOOLEY: When was the last time you saw Tracy Warner?

> *Jared stops dead, sits again. He glances through the glass wall to find Kemel, Davo and Scottie in a silent sullen huddle. Jared looks down at the table.*

JARED: She was …

> *He swallows.*

She was ... dancing.

WILANSKY: With who?

JARED: Some of the girls. Some of the guys. I don't really remember ...

GILHOOLEY: And later in the night? You never saw her?

JARED: I kind of went off ... on my own.

GILHOOLEY: Left your own party?

JARED: I wasn't in a party mood. My girlfriend couldn't come.

WILANSKY: Rachel Ackland?

He looks up in astonishment, then nods.

She was there, son. She found Tracy's body. While she was out looking for you.

{Jared stares at Wilansky.}

SCENE 75 EXT. THE ACKLAND HOUSE – THE HILL. AFTERNOON. {66}

Jared strides up this hilly street of opulent houses overlooking the ocean.

SCENE 76 EXT. THE ACKLAND HOUSE – THE HILL. AFTERNOON. {67}

The front door opens. Stewart sees the boy waiting nervously on his doorstep. He surveys him in cool silence.

JARED: Is she okay?

STEWART: What do you think?

JARED: Can I see her?

Stewart is aware of Marian in the hall behind him, peering at the stranger on the doorstep.

STEWART: She's sleeping. No-one here got much rest last night.

JARED: Could I wait till she ... ?

STEWART: Jesus, son! Have you any idea of the state she's in?

JARED: Just tell her ... tell her I came over.

Stewart nods curtly. Jared turns away. The front door closes behind him.

SCENE 77 EXT. THE KIRBY HOUSE – BLACKROCK. EARLY EVENING. {68}

Jared turns into his street and sees Ricko's van parked outside his house. He pulls up by the driver's window. Ricko smokes.

RICKO: I just missed you at the cop shop. Where the fuck did you get to?

> *Jared shrugs.*

They give you heaps?

> *Jared nods.*

Me too. Pricks. Let's go and get some waves.

> *Jared's face floods with relief.*

SCENE 78 INT./EXT. THE BACK VERANDAH – THE KIRBY HOUSE. EARLY EVENING. {69}

Jared dons his wetsuit. Diane pulls open the sliding doors.

DIANE: They kept you a bloody long time. What was that all about?
JARED: What do you reckon?
DIANE: Well, I was worried, mate ...

> *Beyond her, the TV news shows an aerial view of police scouring the beach. She and Jared turn to it.*

NEWSCASTER: [*voice over*] ... Just below this rocky headland, at around midnight last night, fifteen-year-old Tracy Warner was raped and killed during a teenage party ...

> *She turns down the sound. He reaches for his board.*

DIANE: What about tea?

> *He sees the table beyond her, set for a meal.*

JARED: I'm not hungry.
DIANE: I really need to talk to you.

> *The TV flickers in the background.*

JARED: I got nothing to say.

> *He takes his board and heads off. She follows him out.*

Above left to right: Essie Davis as Det. Gilhooley, Laurence Breuls as Jared and Chris Haywood as Det. Sgt Wilansky. Below: Laurence Breuls as Jared and Simon Lyndon as Ricko. Photos: Elise Lockwood.

SCENE 79 EXT. THE YARD AND DRIVEWAY – THE KIRBY HOUSE. EARLY EVENING.   {70}

DIANE: Not about that.

> *He heads up the driveway and through the side gate, piling into Ricko's van. He sees her standing in the driveway. As Ricko pulls away she heads back inside.*

SCENE 80 INT. THE LIVING ROOM – THE KIRBY HOUSE. EARLY EVENING.   {71}

Diane clears the settings off the table. She glances towards the {silent }TV. {A police officer is being interviewed. As she picks up the remote} Ken Warner appears on the screen, {voiceless though shouting,} standing at his door. And an angry Diane turns a hose on the camera.

SCENE 81 EXT. 'OUT THE BACK' – BLACKROCK BEACH. DUSK.   {72}

A strong nor-easter, a heavy swell. Only Jared, Ricko and a few diehards are still out. Ricko cuts back into a big wave, then dives off the board with casual grace. The board spins. He reclaims it in the surging water. Jared watches in admiration, oblivious now of anything but the moment and the surf.

{SCENE 82 EXT. THE SURF CLUB CAR PARK – BLACKROCK. SUNSET.

Ricko's van is parked, its doors open. Jared's board is propped against it. Under the lamp post, on an improvised work bench, Ricko works intently with an electric sander, shaping a new surfboard. Jared helps. A power cable runs out of the club house.

KEMEL: [*out of view*] Got any gear, Ricko?

> *They turn to find Kemel and Davo on their bikes.*

RICKO: Glove box.

> *Kemel opens the front door of the van. Jared picks up his board and wetsuit. He avoids meeting Kemel and Davo's eyes.*

JARED: Got to get to work.

Jared slopes off into the twilight. Kemel gets a bag of dope from the glove-box. He rolls a joint. His hands shake.

RICKO: Chill out, man.

Kemel glances at Davo, his expression edgy.

DAVO: Mate … it's about Scottie.
KEMEL: We're scared he might do something dumb.
DAVO: He might dob. About Tracy …

Ricko's attention is on his new board.

We did it.
RICKO: You topped her?
DAVO: No! No way. That could have been anyone. Some fuckin' psycho …
KEMEL: Shit, it could have been Kirby.

Ricko laughs easily, working on.

RICKO: Jared? Get real, Camel.
KEMEL: He tried to con on to Tracy. Then we never seen him all night. Did you see him? Eh?
RICKO: You're fuckin' serious! Get out of here. You start paying out on Jared …
KEMEL: Look how he was just now!
RICKO: Fuck off.

He pushes Kemel away.

DAVO: Kemel, back off! He didn't mean it, Ricko. Shit, whoever it was, we went through her.
KEMEL: Fuckin' Toby Ackland started it.
DAVO: Yeah. But we're in it with him.
RICKO: Not if you keep your mouth shut.
DAVO: I reckon we ought to piss off —
KEMEL: No, mate!
DAVO: While we can. Don't you reckon, Ricko? Don't you? Oh, shit. Shit. I bet you know somewhere, some beach you been to —

He's losing it.

KEMEL: Shut the fuck up! Ricko? Straighten him out, man.

Ricko takes Davo by the shoulders and lays a hand on his forehead, almost tenderly. He beckons Kemel into the huddle.

RICKO: Listen to me, both of youse. You know what you got to do? Wipe everything you know about last night.
DAVO: It's not that easy, mate.

He walks them towards the beach.

RICKO: It is. You can make yourself do anything, if you've got the guts.

He points to the dark, silent beach, the headland. The light has nearly gone.

Look. Nothing there for a man to be scared of. Just a rock and a stretch of sand. Okay? Okay.

Ricko turns the sander on, and goes back to work. The two boys slide away into the night.}

SCENE 83 AN OLD-STYLE HAMBURGER JOINT. NIGHT {76}

Davo and Kemel cluster in a booth smoking, murmuring to a frightened Scottie, the remains of food in front of them. Jared cleans up behind the counter, wearing a grungy apron. {The proprietor scrapes the hot-plate. A woman with a baby sits at a table in the corner, reading a Sunday tabloid.} A customer enters quietly, heads for the cigarette machine. Jared notices the three anxious boys freeze as they see the man: Ken Warner. He seems dazed. He fumbles for change, drops it. Jared picks it up. (Note: in the finished film Davo and Kemel don't appear in this scene.)

KEN: Jared …

Jared gives him his change. Ken inserts it.

I roll my own. Can't do it today …

He bangs the machine. A packet of Marlboro emerges.

JARED: Mr Warner … I'm real sorry …

Ken takes the cigarettes, rips them open. {He borrows the woman's lighter. He stares at the baby girl, then turns back to Jared.}

KEN: Police can't get a word out of anyone. No-one knows a bloody thing.

The three boys are on their way out. Kemel and Davo keep their eyes averted. But Scottie stares at Ken, then hurries out to catch his mates.

I bet you feel crook. Your party, and everything …

Ken goes out the door. Jared closes the door after him.

SCENE 84 EXT. THE ROAD OUT OF BLACKROCK. NIGHT.{77}

A boy tries to flag a lift. Cars pass without stopping. Scottie, anxious, looks into oncoming headlights. The car is a police vehicle. It pulls up. Scottie breaks into a desperate run. A young detective gives chase, tackles him by the roadside.

SCENE 85 EXT. BLACKROCK WHARF. MORNING.   {73}

Jared in uniform walks towards the little shed, sees Kemel, Gary and Jason surveying the large black letters daubed across it: 'Dobbers Die'. Davo turns up, sees the slogan. He and Kemel huddle together.

{JASON: Where's Scottie?

Kemel and Davo shrug. But their anxiety shows. Shana and Cherie arrive, see the warning. They avoid the boys and hurry into the shed.}

{SCENE 86   INT./EXT. THE FERRY. MORNING.

The Blacko kids travel in silence. The girls stay in a tight bunch. Cherie, Shana and Leanne keep their eyes downcast. Jared sits apart. Kemel and Davo pass him in silence. Adult commuters look sourly at the boys. Jason stares back.

JASON: What's your problem? Reckon we all got AIDS, or something?

Jared glances at the window beside him. Scrawled on the glass in red marker pen: 'TRACY SLUT'. He glances round. Nobody is looking. He starts rubbing at it with his thumb, then the sleeve of his shirt, breaking off when he sees Cherie staring at him. He pulls his hand away. She sees: 'TRACY SLUT'. The ferry has docked. Cherie looks at him with blazing hatred. He opens his mouth. She hurries off after Jason and the guys. He looks at the mark, rubs at it. It won't budge.}

SCENE 87 EXT. THE TOWN WHARF. MORNING.   {74}

Jared discovers a TV crew shooting their arrival. Jason is being quizzed by an over-styled female interviewer.

JASON: [*pointing to the adult commuters*] They're all looking at us.   They reckon some of us must have done it just cause we were there …

> *Jared pushes through the crowd of kids.   He hears the interviewer turns to another kid.*

INTERVIEWER: Were you at the party? Did you see anything?

> *Jared strides to the street.*

SCENE 88 INT. THE DARK ROOM – THE HIGH SCHOOL. DAY.   {75}

In the dim red light Jared develops pictures from the party.   An image slowly emerges … Tracy at the party, waving her bell towards Jared and his camera.

{SCENE 89   EXT. CENTRAL POLICE STATION – THE CITY. NIGHT.

It's a bigger and more imposing building than the Blackrock station.   All its lights blaze.

SCENE 90 INT. A HALLWAY – CENTRAL POLICE STATION. NIGHT.

Davo is brought down a hallway by two detectives …

SCENE 91 INT. THE MUSTER ROOM – CENTRAL POLICE STATION. NIGHT.

… Into a room full of desks, cops, phones.   He discovers Kemel huddled in one corner, Scottie in another, with a female social worker sitting beside him.   Then he is led into a room where Wilansky and Gilhooley wait.   The door closes behind Davo.   Scottie and Kemel exchange fearful glances across the busy space.}

SCENE 92 EXT. THE SURF CLUB CAR PARK – BLACKROCK. NIGHT. {87}

Under the lamp-post, beside his van, Ricko puts the finishing touches to the sleek new surfboard. It's a beautiful thing. Jared admires it. Charlie the caretaker passes out of the dark club, locking up. He rolls up Ricko's extension lead and gives it to him. The older man sees the board, whistles in admiration, pats Ricko on the back and goes off to his car with a wave to Jared.

RICKO: You like it?
JARED: It's a statement.

> *Ricko looks bemused, then laughs.*

RICKO: Whatever you say, mate. Anyway … it's yours.
JARED: Mate … It's unreal. But … you put all this work into it.
RICKO: Make another one. Got heaps of time. Nothing else, but heaps of time, eh?

> *Jared stares at the new board in awe.*

SCENE 93 INT. DIANE'S ROOM – THE ACKLAND HOUSE. NIGHT. {78}

Diane reads in bed. She hears a key turning, footsteps in the hall. She puts down her book, glances at the bedside clock: 12.30 a.m. Beside it stands the photo of a younger Jared.

DIANE: Jared?

> *No answer. She hears the toilet flush, a door slam.*

SCENE 94 EXT. BLACKROCK CEMETERY. MORNING. {79}

A windswept graveyard by the sea is crowded with family, school principal and teachers, and Tracy's schoolmates. A minister stands by the coffin, with Lesley, Ken, Tracy's sister and relatives. Diane and Glenys stand near Lesley. Jared watches the coffin lowered into the ground. He grimaces as a pop song floats on the air. Lesley keens. Ken shudders uncontrollably as he scatters earth on the coffin. Mourners line up to pay their respects. Jared stands impassive with Gary, Jason and other Blacko guys. Only Gary is crying. Rachel, weeping, leaves Toby's side and joins the line. Jared's glassy eyes, showing the world nothing, reflect …

SCENE 95 EXT. NEAR THE HEADLAND – BLACKROCK
BEACH. NIGHT.   {80}

Tracy staggers to her feet, desolate in the moonlight.

SCENE 96 EXT. BLACKROCK CEMETERY. MORNING. {81, 82}

Cherie and her girlfriends sob as they throw earth and flowers in the grave. Diane passes Jared. She makes a gap in the line of mourners. Gary steps out from the group of boys. This provokes frowns, a murmur of disapproval. Jared stays in the group of boys. He looks up as the news helicopter passes overhead. (Note: in the finished film the helicopter is treated as a separate scene.)

SCENE 97 EXT. BLACKROCK CEMETERY – THE STREET.
MORNING.   {83}

Mourners leave the burial. The Warners are steered past a camera crew and hustled into a car, which moves off. Diane and Glenys follow in Glenys's old bomb. Jared waits by the gate. Jason passes him, murmuring …

JASON: Mate … where's Camel? And Davo?

> *Jared shrugs. They see Rachel approaching. Jason moves away. Jared puts a tentative arm round her.*

RACHEL: It feels like about a year since I've seen you. Everything's so weird …

> *They see Toby cross the street to the Volvo. A man in a dark suit approaches Toby, who begins to panic. After a few words, Toby follows him to a waiting car.*

RACHEL: Oh, God …

> *Suddenly, a loud cry across the street.*

SHANA: No! No way!

> *Shana and Jason fight in a clump of kids. Shana cries in rage. She hits him. He hits back.*

JASON: She was a fuckin' slag!

Cherie pushes through the clump of boys round Jason. She's a virago, yelling, clawing, kicking. The kids could do serious damage to each other. Gary tries to restrain Jason. The news crew sprints in to catch the fight. By the cemetery fence Jared stares at the fight. Rachel tugs at his arm.

RACHEL: Do something! Jared!

He's motionless as the brawl escalates.

SCENE 98 EXT. THE SCHOOLYARD. DAY.   {84}

Ranks of silent schoolkids addressed by the principal, a middle-aged man. Teachers group around him.

PRINCIPAL: … This is no way to pay respect to a dead schoolmate.

{*He looks down the ranks, past Jason, his face scratched …*}

We need to give everyone time to get over this terrible business …

{*… Leanne, shaken and tearful, Shana, clear-eyed and mutinous …*}

… But as a school, we need to move on, now —
SHANA: We need to do something for Tracy.

{*Silence. The Principal looks for the source of the voice. Cherie steps out of the line.*}

CHERIE: Something round here to remember her.

Guys groan loudly. {*Jared, silent, stares at Cherie who walks forward to the front of the assembly.*}

To show what we think about her.

{*Shana follows her.*}

SHANA: What the girls think, anyway.

Boys mutter. {*The principal calls for order. The girls reach the front. They turn to the students.*}

CHERIE: We should plant a tree.

The yard erupts.

SCENE 99 EXT. A COVERED WALKWAY – THE
SCHOOLYARD. DAY.   {85}

Rain falls. Jared walks past huddles of schoolkids sheltering from the weather and processing the day's rumours. Jason stands with Blacko guys:

JASON: Cops have grabbed Kemel and Scottie and Davo …

A group of Blackrock girls:

GIRL: Can't have been those guys. Spider seen this black panel van with Victorian number-plates …

A group of younger boys:

BOY: Scottie saw the murder. He had to piss off cause he knows too much …

A group of town guys:

TOWN GUYS: Has to have been a psycho. They let them out anywhere now …

Jared strides past them, out into the rain to find Cherie collecting money in a bucket.

JARED: Cherie, wake up to yourself.
CHERIE: Mind your own business!

Rachel arrives with another bucket.

JARED: You know what'll happen? Same as the funeral, same as the ferry. You'll plant a tree, and a TV crew will be all over us like flies, paying out on Blackrock: the hoons over the water …
RACHEL: Don't be so pathetic.

He grabs her bucket. She holds onto it.

JARED: Someone died and you think you'll make it better by planting a fuckin' tree. That's pathetic.

Cherie and Rachel pull at the bucket.

RACHEL: It's better than saying nothing and feeling nothing —
JARED: Don't fuckin' tell me what I'm feeling!

Jared hurls the bucket to the ground, scattering the money. {The girls scrabble for the coins. The bell rings. Outside the admin building, Jared passes a crew shooting an interview with the principal on the steps. Jared heads out of the yard and down the hill.}

{SCENE 100 INT. THE HALL – THE NURSING-HOME. DAY.

Diane in her smock dispenses tea to the residents. A group sit chatting. As she reaches them they stop and stare.

OLD WOMAN: How was the funeral?

> *Diane shrugs, smiles, pours tea.*

OLD MAN: What was she like, the little girl?
OLD WOMAN: No better than she should have been, by the sound of her.

> *Diane's smile hardens.*

DIANE: Reckon we'd all like people to think the best of us after we're gone. Wouldn't we?

> *She moves on, angry. The conversation follows her.*

OLD WOMAN: A real little sleeparound …}

SCENE 101 EXT. THE SHORE-LINE – BLACKROCK BEACH. AFTERNOON.   {88}

Jared in his wetsuit brings his new board onto the beach. He sees two people walking along the shore-line: Ken Warner, with his arm round Lesley. She holds a little posy of flowers. They're heading towards the rock. Lesley sees him, makes a small wave. The couple move on. Jared watches them go. He heads gratefully for the water. Good waves. A few surfers out the back. Jared paddles out.

SCENE 102 INT. A SUBURBAN GYMNASIUM. AFTERNOON.{86}

Diane sees athletes working out. An old bloke at the desk studies a form guide.

DIANE: I wanted to see Mr Kirby.

> *He glances across the space. Two sweating young boxers spar: a Koori, Jimmy, and a Slav, George. Len Kirby, a burly, handsome man of forty-five, coaches.*

OLD BLOKE: [*calling*] Lennie?

Len looks. Diane approaches. George and Jimmy gawp at Diane, the only woman in the space. Len snaps at them.

LEN: Did I say stop?

They go back to sparring.

DIANE: I need to talk to you.

He points to the boys in training.

I'm due back at work. I'll be quick.

Len opens a stick of gum, starts to chew.

LEN: Nicorets. Taste like shit. I'd rather get cancer.

He offers her a chair.

I'm not sending any more dough.
DIANE: That's not what I want. I need you to come and see Jared.
LEN: Boy knows where to find me.
DIANE: Boy? He's tall as you now.
LEN: Got himself a job?
DIANE: He's staying on for his HSC.

Len glances at the idle boxers.

LEN: Send him round. I'll take him out for a drink.
DIANE: You know he won't come, Len. He's too angry.
LEN: Wonder where he got that from?

She goes to snap back, bites her tongue. A boxer runs into the gym, breathless. Len looks at his watch. The boxer mutters apologies, runs to the change-room.

DIANE: Right now he needs … I dunno, a bit of guidance.
LEN: You'd never be backward with that.
DIANE: What if something happens to me?

He snorts.

LEN: Give me a break!
DIANE: I could go under a bus tomorrow. Anyway … he needs a man, Len.
LEN: I thought you'd have nailed some other poor prick by now.

Her eyes flash. He grins.

LEN: Joke.

DIANE: He needs his Dad. You haven't been near him in ... how long?
LEN: I took him to Seal Rocks for Christmas —
DIANE: Two years ago, and spent the whole time shut up with Rhonda in the caravan. Since then, not so much as a birthday card.
LEN: You haven't learnt a thing, have you? Exactly the fuckin' same ...

The boxers stare. Diane moves away. They both calm down. He puts a hand on her shoulder.

Look, what can I do for him now? He's nearly a man.
DIANE: But what kind of a man's he going to be? Please, Len.
LEN: Send him over. I'll do what I can.

He calls the boys back to the ring.

Teach him to look after himself, anyway.

He waves and goes back to work. Diane leaves. She passes a young woman, Rhonda, with a toddler and a baby in a stroller, coming through the street doors.

SCENE 103 EXT. ON THE WATER – BLACKROCK BEACH. AFTERNOON. {89}

Jared pushes through the surf, sitting up on his board. He turns towards the shore and sees, beyond it, the industrial skyline, the belching chimneys of the city. His face is troubled, angry. He lets himself slip off the board, and sinks into ...

SCENE 104 EXT. UNDER WATER – BLACKROCK BEACH. AFTERNOON. {90}

A calm and silent world. Jared floats at peace, as though suspended. He watches his own air bubbles. His limbs move slowly, easily; his hair floats. No-one can reach him here in this nether world. The sun's rays shaft down through the water. The sky is a dim pale dome. Life seems to have come to an end.

{SCENE 105 INT. STEWART'S OFFICE – ACKLAND ADVERTISING AGENCY. AFTERNOON.

A large blow-up of the models on the pile of debris: bare skin, white underwear in a ruined landscape. The table covered in blow-ups. Stewart in shirtsleeves cracks pistachios. Leesha finds a shot of her in the high doorway.

LEESHA: Art-house stuff.
STEWART: What would you go for?

> *She takes up a mid-shot of her in bra and bikini briefs, with a muscular guy in workshorts holding her. She applies a large pair of scissors.*

LEESHA: Splatter movie ...

> *She cuts off sections of the photo, producing two headless figures. She holds it up: two beautiful torsos in underwear.*

Now all you look at is the product.

> *He laughs and cracks a nut.*

Test it. You'll see.

> *A knock on the door. A secretary ushers in Marian, distressed.}*

SCENE 106 EXT. THE ACKLAND HOUSE – THE STREET. AFTERNOON. {91}

Rachel in uniform walks up the hill with her bag. She sees Jared, out of uniform, hovering on his bike opposite the house. He gets up. She stops at her front gate. He keeps his distance.

JARED: I was a real dick today.

> *Surprised, she stands in silence.*

You been through enough shit already. Sorry.

> *They stand in awkward silence.*

Are your olds home?
RACHEL: Doesn't look like it.

> *She sees the naked need in his eyes.*

SCENE 107 INT. THE LIVING ROOM – THE ACKLAND HOUSE. AFTERNOON. {92}

He follows her into the living-room, sees a spectacular ocean vista. She hovers awkwardly. He tries to put his arms around her. She resists.

JARED: I'd just like to ...
RACHEL: I can't ... It doesn't feel right.
JARED: Nothing does.

He walks to the window, looks out to sea.

I just want ... I dunno.
RACHEL: They sent me to a counsellor ... It's so weird. She has a fish-tank in her office. She asked me say whatever came into my head. I said one of your fish is dead.

They both try to laugh, then stand in silence.

What do you want? Jared? Tell me.
JARED: I want it to be last week. I feel crook in the guts all the time. I can't sleep.
RACHEL: I don't want to sleep. Because then I start dreaming. Seeing ... her and those guys ...

He looks away.

Look, I'm sorry, but you weren't ... you know ... involved ... were you? Jared?

She holds her breath.

JARED: No! I didn't do anything!
RACHEL: Okay.

He paces the room wildly.

RACHEL: It's okay, Jared.
JARED: No, it's not! I didn't do anything. You hear what I'm saying? I didn't do anything.

The front door opens. Stewart and Marian come in, both distressed.

RACHEL: Mum ... What's up?

Marian is unable to speak. She turns away.

STEWART: You'd better go home, son.

Jared slides off.

{RACHEL: What is it?}

SCENE 108 INT. THE LIVING ROOM – THE MILENKO HOUSE. EARLY EVENING.   {93}

Cherie stares at the TV, on which teenage boys, faces obscured, are led to a police van.

NEWSCASTER: [*voice over*] … The youths have been charged with sexual assault and held in custody until a date is set for a committal hearing …

Glenys appears, looking at the screen … then at Cherie.

CHERIE: Craig Davidson … Kemel Ayoub … Scottie Blaylock …

On screen, the last of the boys enters the van.

CHERIE: Toby Ackland …

{SCENE 109   EXT. A STREET – BLACKROCK. EARLY EVENING.

Jared pounds his way down the street. Every TV in every house seems to resonate with the news. Fragments of reports and interviews assail him on all sides: Jason, defiant on the ferry wharf:

JASON: Anyone could have done it.

A stylish woman interviewer:

INTERVIEWER: It's not known whether the youths will also be charged over Tracy Warner's death …

Ken and Lesley Warner at their front door:

KEN: Prison's too good for them. I say a life for a life …

Imploding in fury, Jared sees a home-made poster taped to a telegraph pole: a photo of Tracy over the legend, 'SHAME, BLACKROCK, SHAME' …}

SCENE 110 INT. THE LIVING ROOM – THE KIRBY HOUSE. EARLY EVENING.   {94}

Jared comes in to find Diane watching the TV. {On the screen, Shana and Jason brawl at the funeral.} *Jared heads for his room. She follows him down the hall.*

DIANE: Jared ...

SCENE 111 INT. JARED'S ROOM – THE KIRBY HOUSE. EARLY EVENING. {95}

He searches near Ricko's photo flanked by the trophies.

DIANE: I know, I'm spinning out too.

He finds a card, puts it in his pocket.

Those boys have been in and out of this house for years. And they're killers.
JARED: They're not.
DIANE: Bloody well looks like it.
JARED: Mum, they didn't kill her.
DIANE: How would you know?
JARED: I just know.
DIANE: Well, do you know who did?

He shakes his head.

I'm a bit slow, sorry. You know your mates didn't do it, but you don't know who did? How come?
JARED: I just know.
DIANE: Did you tell the police? {I bet you didn't. Dobbers die, eh?

He gropes in his bag, finds a couple of cigarettes in a crushed box.

Be an idea to tell them now ...}

He heads into the hall. The phone starts ringing.

{If you're that worried about your mates, open your mouth, say something ...
JARED: All right! I'm going! Fuck ...}

He goes out the front door. She picks up the phone.

DIANE: This is her ... Tomorrow? Oh. What time?

She listens to the instructions.

Is there a ward number, or ... ? {Thank you.

Laurence Breuls as Jared. Photo: Elise Lockwood.

She hangs up, writes down the instructions. She takes a moment to calm herself, then hurries out the door.}

SCENE 112 EXT. A STREET – BLACKROCK. EARLY EVENING.{96}

Diane reaches the corner, breathless. A young girl passes on a bike.

DIANE: Did you see Jared, Tamsin?

The girl shakes her head and rides on. A car passes, slows down, honks. Glenys is the driver.

GLENYS: I've lost Cherie. Little bugger saw the news and took off …

She peers out at Diane.

You okay?

Diane nods. Glenys looks wryly at her.

Sure you are. Get in. {Diane, get in!

She opens the door. Diane gets in.}

SCENE 113 EXT. AYOUB LEBANESE TAKEAWAY – BLACKROCK. EARLY EVENING   {97}

Cherie, panting, reaches the shop. She picks up a soft-drink bottle and hurls it at the front window. It bounces off. She scrabbles through a garbage can, showering the window with stones and rubbish. Mr Ayoub runs out as she picks up the bin. He wrestles with it. Cherie drops it, sprints down the street. Glenys's car approaches. She sees Mr Ayoub yelling at her disappearing daughter, Mrs Ayoub cleaning up the footpath.

{SCENE 114   INT./ EXT. THE FERRY. EARLY EVENING

Jared crosses towards town. He looks to the looming lights of the city. He stands, lurching as the boat docks. He puts his last cigarette in his mouth.

SCENE 115 INT. THE DINING ROOM – THE ACKLAND HOUSE. NIGHT.

Takeaway food. No table setting on the polished granite top. Marian and Stewart look at Rachel, who doesn't eat.

STEWART: Sweetie … Toby did something pretty stupid, pretty bad. But he's not a killer. Mum and I believe that. Do you?

Rachel nods slowly.

But she died, and everything else will be judged that much more harshly. Now, if you saw the girl … Did you see her?

Rachel starts to cry.

Christ! I meant beforehand, during the party. If you saw anything …

Marian puts an arm round Rachel. She signals to Stewart to leave them. He speaks quietly, almost mumbling …

Please help Toby if you can. It was sex, Rachel, nothing more …

She doesn't look up. He goes.

RACHEL: They left her down on the beach. What if she'd drowned?

Marian clears the plates.

MARIAN: Don't you think she might have brought it on herself? Through drugs or alcohol, or … just being careless? If you noticed anything earlier in the night …

Rachel glances at her, then looks down.

You did, didn't you?

Slowly, Rachel nods. Marian sits with her.}

SCENE 116 EXT. CENTRAL POLICE STATION – THE CITY. NIGHT.   {98}

Jared reaches the pathway to the front door. He braces himself, then walks towards the building … as Ricko emerges. Both stop in surprise.

RICKO: They call you in too?

Jared shakes his head. He goes towards the station. Ricko follows.

JARED: Don't hang round for me. Reckon I might be a while.
RICKO: Doing what?
JARED: Got to talk to someone.
RICKO: What about?
JARED: Might be able to help Kemel and Davo and them, sort of.
RICKO: Bit late, mate. They confessed. They all went through her.
JARED: But after …

Ricko grabs his arm, draws him round the side of the building, away from the ground-floor windows.

Cops know they didn't top her.
JARED: You sure?

Ricko puts an arm round Jared. He looks troubled.

RICKO: They're trying to hang it on me.

He walks towards his van, parked in a side street. Jared follows him. Ricko lights a cigarette.

JARED: Bullshit.
RICKO: Try and tell them that …

Jared takes Ricko's cigarettes, helps himself to one.

I told them I was with you.

He leans against the van, smoking. Jared stares at him.

SCENE 117 EXT. BLACKROCK CEMETERY. NIGHT.   {99}

Cherie hugs her knees to her chest. A breeze blows.

CHERIE: It's not right. Nothing can make it right. Whatever happens to them four …

She is kneeling by Tracy's grave. There's no tombstone yet, just a cross and marker. She has a boom box beside her.

… They'll still be alive and you'll still be dead.

She feels a torch-beam, sees Glenys staring at her. Diane hovers behind her.

GLENYS: Do I have to chain you up like a dog?

Cherie turns away, staring at the rough cross.

Grounded means grounded, Cherie. Get in the car. On the way home you'll go in to the Ayoubs and apologise. None of it was their fault.

CHERIE: Nothing's anybody's fault. She raped herself. She killed herself. That's what youse all think.

GLENYS: Tell you what I think ...

CHERIE: I don't want to know.

She moves away. Glenys calls across the grave.

GLENYS: If you douse yourself in kero, then start playing with matches, you can't blame anyone else when you set yourself on fire.

CHERIE: Shut up!

She swings at Glenys, who catches her arm. Diane tries to restrain them.

GLENYS: Don't raise your hand to your own mother.

CHERIE: You're not! Not if you say that about Tracy. And here, where she can hear you ...

Glenys lets Cherie go.

GLENYS: She can hear me ... ?

She studies Cherie silently. Cherie stares defiantly back.

You think she can hear you?

Cherie nods.

And talk to you?

Cherie looks guarded now.

DIANE: Let it go, Glenys.

GLENYS: I hope she can, Cherie. So she can tell you not to be the bloody idiot she was.

Cherie dives for her mother. Diane restrains her.

CHERIE: Take it back!

GLENYS: It's true. I want you alive!

Cherie's anger is giving way to tears, which she resists. She breaks from Diane and runs away through the headstones. {The girl is at the edge of the

graveyard overlooking the ocean. Beyond her,} the two women stand by
Tracy's grave. Glenys sits, turning away from Diane.*

All right, say it.

DIANE: Well, it was a bit rough.

GLENYS: Shut up.

DIANE: You asked.

GLENYS: You're not bringing up a girl. Jared can take care of himself.
Cherie's got to learn the way the world works.

Diane studies the wooden marker.

DIANE: No, Glen.

Glenys looks at her sharply.

She's right.

*Glenys snorts, takes out her cigarettes. They find themselves looking at the
grave.*

Nobody should have to die before their time. It's just ... It's not
fair.

She walks through the graves. Glenys catches up with her.

GLENYS: What's up?

She holds her by the arm.

For Christ's sake ...

DIANE: I'm crook. And I'm scared.

She puts a hand on her left breast.

They're going to take this off tomorrow.

Glenys takes a deep breath.

GLENYS: Thanks for telling me.

DIANE: I've told nobody.

GLENYS: Not even Jared?

Diane shakes her head.

And I'm the one that gets the lecture ...

DIANE: I've tried, sort of. I don't want to come unstuck.

GLENYS: You got to say something before tomorrow. What if ... ?

She stops herself. They both know the sentence can't be finished. Music drifts across the cemetery. At Tracy's grave Cherie plays a song.

Girl's going to end up in the loony-bin.

She strides off towards her daughter. Diane rips up weeds from a grave.

SCENE 118 EXT. ROCKS AND OCEAN BATHS – A CITY BEACH. NIGHT. {100}

Jared and Ricko sit on a rail on the footpath outside the van, looking out to sea. Ricko swigs a bottle of tequila. He offers the bottle to Jared, who shakes his head.

JARED: I already told them I was on my own.

RICKO: You were that ripped you forgot. Now you remember: Ricko was there.

Jared walks away towards the wall of the ocean baths.

And if we back each other up …

JARED: Mate … I'm a shit-house liar. Just tell them what really happened.

RICKO: They could just as easy pin it on you. You and Ackland had a fight over Tracy. You were hot for her. Ackland scored. You hung round, waiting for your chance.

JARED: Bullshit. I was on my own all night.

RICKO: No-one saw you.

JARED: Nothing to see. I didn't do it! I didn't kill her.

RICKO: I know you didn't! I did.

Jared turns, looks deep into his mate's eyes, sees something new there: fear. He turns away from it, and bolts. Ricko catches him, forces him against the wooden railing.

JARED: Back off!

Jared is fitter, but Ricko is wilder. Jared falls against the rail, tumbling over. Ricko straddles him.

Get off me, you bastard!

They roll across the concrete, landing on the sand. Jared is winded, his T-shirt ripped and stained. He attacks Ricko, smashing him in the face. Ricko reels back in shock. Blood runs from his nose.

You asked for that. Just back off!

He runs along the beach, eerily lit by the high fluoros lining the concrete promenade. Suddenly Jared is barrelled from behind. Ricko rolls him in the sand, straddles his chest. Jared sees blood dripping onto his T-shirt from Ricko's nose. He howls in disgust. Ricko pins his arms down.

RICKO: Have you lost it or what?

JARED: Let me up.

He struggles, powerless against Ricko's force. The blood keeps dripping down onto him. Jared gags.

Shit, that went in my mouth!

Ricko unpins his arms. Jared fights. Ricko pins him again.

RICKO: Will you listen to me?

Jared stops resisting. Ricko lets go Jared's arms.

I didn't mean it. I only wanted to pound her. Things got rough, she hit her head on a rock, and she was gone. That quick.

Jared can't look up at Ricko.

Think they'd buy that? Think they'd believe a hoon like me? I said I was with my mate. I knew you'd be there for me.

Jared shakes his head. Ricko gets off him.

Fuck you. I thought you were the one …

Jared gets up, wiping Ricko's blood off his face.

… The one who'd stick by me.

Jared walks away, checking his bruises. Ricko recedes behind him, his voice mingling with the sound of the waves on the rocks beyond.

I'd be there for you. You know I would.

Jared stops, a long way from Ricko on the silent beach.

JARED: You swear you didn't mean to do it?

Ricko comes slowly towards him, wiping his nose on his sleeve. Jared sees a glint of tears in his eyes.

RICKO: It was that quick I don't even remember.

Jared walks down to the water, taking off his T-shirt. He stands in the shallows and dips it in the surf. He wipes himself off, and throws the sodden rag to Ricko.

{SCENE 119 INT. THE KITCHEN – THE KIRBY HOUSE. NIGHT.

Diane scrubs out the oven, the floor covered in newspaper. The stove top gleams. She rinses the rag in the spotless sink. A cop show plays on TV in the next room. She straightens up, easing her back. Her old T-shirt is covered in grease and stains, her hair tied in a drab scarf, hands in rubber gloves. She hears the front door-bell. She empties the overflowing kitchen-tidy into a bin …}

SCENE 120 INT/ EXT. THE FRONT DOOR – THE KIRBY HOUSE. NIGHT.   {101}

… And opens the front door, bin in hand. Geoff is there with a bottle in a paper bag. He takes in her daggy appearance, grins.

GEOFF: Thought you might feel like a Christmas drink.
DIANE: Bit early. How'd you find out my address?
GEOFF: Great new invention called the phone book …
DIANE: You remembered my last name?
GEOFF: Remembered quite a few things. Can I come in?

She indicates the bin in her hand.

DIANE: I'm a bit busy.
GEOFF: Take a little break.

He reaches for the garbage bin.

DIANE: Look … [*groping for the name*] Geoff …

He smiles, offers the bottle.

GEOFF: {Bingo.} You going to ask me in?
DIANE: I'm going away tomorrow. And I've got a lot to get through tonight.
GEOFF: Maybe next weekend? Can I give you a call?

She hesitates.

I thought we sort of hit it off.

She smiles briefly, wanly ...

DIANE: Yeah. We did. But ... it was just a Saturday-night thing, you know? No big deal.

His face darkens.

GEOFF: Sorry to waste your time.

He {dumps the bin outside the front gate and} drives away. She {watches him go, picking up advertising dodgers which litter the ground. She stows them in the bin ... and} sees a police-car cruising towards her, slowing as it reaches the gate. It pulls up. She hears a sound from the house next door. The nosy neighbour, Mrs Lindsay, peers out from her front window.

DIANE: It's okay, Mrs Lindsay, it's only a drug bust.

Diane sees Gilhooley and another detective step from the car.

Don't you people have homes to go to?
GILHOOLEY: Sometimes I can't remember.

{They both react as sounds of gunshots and a car chase float through Diane's open front door on this still summer night.}

Mrs Kirby? Sharon Gilhooley. We'd like to talk to Jared.
DIANE: He's not here.
GILHOOLEY: You're quite sure?
DIANE: No, I'm lying. I've got him tied up in the garage.

Diane feels the younger woman scanning her shabby appearance.

GILHOOLEY: Do you know where Jared is?
DIANE: Do you?

{Diane glances next door, sees Mrs Lindsay and her husband still staring.}

Look, come inside or go away.

She strides into the house with the bin.

SCENE 121 INT. THE LIVING ROOM – THE KIRBY HOUSE. NIGHT.

A commercial break on TV: a Kelloggs family eats breakfast, all with bright clothes and good teeth.

GILHOOLEY: I know all this is hard on the parents. I've got kids myself ...

Diane peels off the rubber gloves.

DIANE: You don't look nearly old enough.
GILHOOLEY: My oldest is nine. She's already up to here on me ...

She holds her palm at breast level. She hands Diane a card.

Jared should call the minute he gets in.

Diane takes the card.

GILHOOLEY: Just some follow-up questions.

Diane turns the card over in her hand. On TV now, a snack-food commercial features a boisterous party.

DIANE: Be a long time before there's another party round here, eh?
GILHOOLEY: Please make sure he calls.
DIANE: I'm not his minder!

They're both startled by her harsh tone.

You caught me on a bad night.

Gilhooley nods, edging her way towards the door.

GILHOOLEY: Doesn't matter how late. We're working round the clock.

SCENE 122 EXT. THE KIRBY HOUSE – THE STREET. NIGHT.

Diane follows Detective Gilhooley out of the house.

DIANE: Is he in strife?

Gilhooley seems immediately guarded.

GILHOOLEY: We need to clarify a few points in his statement.

Gilhooley walks down the path.

DIANE: That's not what I asked.

Gilhooley stops at the gate, might be about to reply, but gets in the car. It drives away.

SCENE 123 INT. JARED'S ROOM – THE KIRBY HOUSE. NIGHT.

Diane opens a drawer, finds Jared's dope stash, papers. She rolls a joint. As she licks the paper, her eye goes to the photographs: Ricko the surfing champ, Rachel grunged down for some party … Smoking, she explores the messy room.   On Jared's desk, among a pile of schoolbooks and folders, she finds a large black folder. She opens it: the 'art file': industrial wasteland, a heap of abandoned car-wrecks … then a family portrait, artfully treated: a blown-up colour snap of Diane, Len and a ten-year-old Jared, fractured and fissured and skewed, applied onto a starkly beautiful black-and-white shot of an empty boxing ring. Diane smokes, studies it … then sees a Kodak box beneath it, opens it to find the party shots printed by Jared: Ricko with Tiffany … Tracy surrounded by Cherie, Leanne and Shana, all clowning … Tracy ringing her bell for the camera.}

SCENE 124 EXT. THE HEADLAND – BLACKROCK. NIGHT.{102}

The embers of a fire glow. The van doors are open. Ricko, Tiffany and Jared drink on the cliff edge. Jared sees a car cruise up the hill. He nudges Ricko, points.

JARED: Mate …

> *Ricko sees and quickly pulls Jared and Tiffany down onto a ledge out of sight.*

TIFFANY: Ricko! What are you – ?

> *Ricko clamps his hand over Tiffany's mouth. She struggles, giggling. She starts to suck his finger. Jared, still speedy, pisses himself. They crouch out of sight, watching the car stop near the van. Two figures get out, approach the van, look in. One is Gilhooley. They shine torches round the headland. {Crouching down below the cliff edge, Ricko starts to kiss Tiffany's neck. She wriggles, letting out a tiny sound. He gags her again, then kisses her on the mouth. Jared watches. Ricko rolls his eyes raunchily at Jared over Tiffany's shoulder as he nuzzles her neck. Jared laughs, then sees the police car driving away.*

You bastard, Ricko!

> *Tiffany starts to slap and punch Ricko, who mock-spars with her, laughing. Jared takes Ricko on, aping Tiffany …*

JARED: You bastard, Ricko!

> *The three of them tussle on the cliff edge.*}

SCENE 125 EXT. BLACKROCK WHARF. DAWN.   {103}

Diane waits with her overnight bag as the ferry chugs towards her in the grey light.

SCENE 126 INT./EXT. MONTAGE.   {107}

Distorted images: Tracy lurching down the beach ... a body on the sand ... a body on a slab or table ... a rock descending.

SCENE 127 INT./EXT. RICKO'S VAN – THE HEADLAND. DAWN.   {108}

Jared jolts awake, sweating. He's on the mattress in the van. Ricko lies beside him, sleeping, the tattoo on his biceps rising and falling with his even breathing ... and curled in a corner of the mattress near the door, her nakedness covered with a blanket, Tiffany. Jared grabs his clothes and stumbles towards the doors.

SCENE 128 INT. A PUBLIC WARD – THE CITY HOSPITAL. MORNING.   {109}

A nurse brings a hospital gown. Diane unpacks her bag, putting a picture on her bedside table: a photo of her and a slightly younger Jared poking faces at a party.

SCENE 129 EXT. SCHOOLYARD. MORNING.   {104}

A spade thrusts into hard soil. Cherie digs a hole in the lawn near the school gates. Near her is a small native tree, its base wrapped in plastic. By the fence, Blacko boys stare in silence. Shana and Leanne carry the tree to the hole. One voice suddenly rings out ...

JASON: Sickos.

> *He moves towards them. He looks wasted but punchy. Gary steps in his path.*

GARY: Get over it, Jason.

Leanne stares coldly at Jason, who pushes Gary aside and rejoins his mates. Shana lowers the tree into the hole. The girls press the soil down. From the office, the principal and teachers watch the ceremony apprehensively. Rachel moves in with a camera. Cherie looks up sharply as Rachel lines up a shot of the three with the tree.

CHERIE: Piss off.
RACHEL: This is important.
CHERIE: Piss off!
RACHEL: Please. I found her.
CHERIE: Yeah, and your brother ...

She stops herself. Rachel lowers the camera.

Trace really liked Toby. She never thought he'd look at her. He was such a hero ...

Cherie breaks off as she sees Jason throw a stone towards the tree. She hurls one back at him. Jason and Gary start to fight. Jason's Blacko mate backs him up. The art teacher hurries into the yard, damping down the fight. She takes up a post between the girls and the boys.

She'd never even done it before.

She sees Rachel's astonishment. She presses the fresh soil round the spindly trunk.

Her first time. And it happened that way ...

Rachel swallows. The boys mutter as Rachel photographs Cherie with the tree.

JASON'S MATE: Lezzos.

Cherie strides to the no-man's-land where the art teacher stands. She looks Jason's mate in the eye.

CHERIE: I'd rather be one of them than go with any of youse.

Gary applauds. Jason hits him. The art teacher intervenes. Cherie joins Leanne and Shana who bring water for the young tree. Rachel looks from them to the street beyond the fence as a BMW pulls up. (Note: in the finished film the following is treated as a new scene.) Stewart and Marian are in the car. Rachel, motionless, stares at them. The bell goes. The kids clear the yard. Stewart leans out of the driver's window. Rachel sees the tree, her school mates returning to class, the boys in one tight group, the girls in another. She walks towards the car.

SCENE 130 INT. A LAWYER'S OFFICE. DAY.   {106}

Rachel, Stewart and Marian sit on one side of a large desk. The lawyer, Mr Kamen, smiles at Rachel.

KAMEN: If we can establish something about Tracy's behaviour on the night …

Rachel sits in silence.

Tell Mr Kamen what you told me.

Rachel looks at her hands.

Rachel. Those three girls, carrying on …
RACHEL: It was a party! They were just mucking round.
MARIAN: That's not the way you told it to me!
RACHEL: I bet they terrified her. Four of them. How could it have been four? She thought Toby was the cool dude, the hero …

She rises.

STEWART: Rachel, do you think your brother's good-looking?

She looks uncertainly at him.

Do you think he's a nice-looking boy?

She nods.

You know what happens to pretty boys in jail?
MARIAN: Stewart, that's enough!
STEWART: I hope so.

He helps himself to water. Rachel looks at the lawyer.

RACHEL: I have to get back to school.
STEWART: You have to say what you saw!
RACHEL: What was the last thing she saw?

She walks out of the room.

SCENE 131 EXT. CENTRAL POLICE STATION – THE CITY. DAY. {110}

Ricko drops Jared off in the van. Jared crosses the street. He looks unkempt, wasted. {He reaches the footpath outside the police station and stops dead. He looks towards the doors.}

{SCENE 132 INT. THE ART-ROOM – THE HIGH SCHOOL. DAY.

Near Jared's half-completed display – the cut-out female figure from the poster, the words 'Body Count' cut out jaggedly, the collage of grunge – Rachel works with concentrated fury, discarding her own display, scattering pictures, mounting instead a vast expanse of black, in its centre a small stark black-and-white photograph: a mound of earth, a grave, a wooden marker, Tracy's name, a single bunch of flowers.}

SCENE 133 EXT. CENTRAL POLICE STATION – THE CITY. DAY. {111}

Jared {hesitates outside the building. Under the high summer sun it seems starker and more massive than last night. He} goes through the doors.

SCENE 134 INT. AN OPERATING THEATRE – THE CITY HOSPITAL. DAY. {112}

Diane goes under anaesthetic.

SCENE 135 INT. AN INTERVIEW ROOM – CENTRAL POLICE STATION. DAY. {113}

{There are beads of sweat on Jared's upper lip.}

JARED: We did a couple of cones. And we ... you know, we raved on.
GILHOOLEY: [*out of view*] What about?
JARED: Heaps of stuff. Photography.
WILANSKY: [*out of view*] How long for, son?

JARED: Probably … about half an hour.

Wilansky pops a Soother into his mouth, offering one to Gilhooley, who shakes her head. Wilansky rounds on Jared.

WILANSKY: Long time to be talking photography.

JARED: I'd like to do it. As a career, I mean. I've really got into it this year. We're putting an exhibition together at school. I told him about that. I've got a chance to do work experience at an advertising agency …

They seem to have lost interest. He falters.

Ricko was pretty impressed.

GILHOOLEY: What did he say? How did he put it?

Jared has no answer for a moment.

WILANSKY: You can remember your side of the conversation.

Jared shrugs. He wipes sweat from his forehead.

GILHOOLEY: Do you think you've got a future? As a photographer?

JARED: Dunno. My teacher says I got a good eye, but … I'm obsessed with grunge.

He tries to smile … but they won't smile back.

GILHOOLEY: Are you a fighter, Jared?

He looks at her in surprise.

JARED: I can look after myself.

WILANSKY: So we hear.

Jared turns to him, jolted by the sharpness of his tone. Wilansky blows his nose hard. The noise resonates.}

You had a fight with Toby Ackland during your party.

JARED: Bit of an argument, that's all.

GILHOOLEY: Over Tracy. He got her, and you didn't. Did that piss you off, Jared?

JARED: How do you mean?

WILANSKY: How do you think she means? Were you angry? Did you go and find Tracy after the others had —

JARED: No! No way!

He sweats, staring at the lens of the video camera.

I was with Ricko.

WILANSKY: Of course you were. You told us that. {And no-one else saw you for the rest of the night.

JARED: I told you, I went straight home! I didn't go back to the club.

WILANSKY: It was your party. Who else was going to close the place up?

JARED: I was out of it! I would have gone back next morning.}

GILHOOLEY: And you didn't see Tracy again after that fight?

JARED: No, I didn't.

GILHOOLEY: So it couldn't have been you that killed her. {Cuts the field down a bit, Jared. Nearly everyone else is accounted for.}

The heat is stifling. Jared reaches for water. Wilansky clears his congested throat. Gilhooley murmurs in his ear ...

You ought to be home in bed, Phil.

WILANSKY: I'll get there. Jared, would you say Brett Ricketson is your best mate?

Jared nods.

He's quite a bit older than you.

JARED: Couple of years.

WILANSKY: Five. Five years.

JARED: He looked after me when I was a kid. Took me under his wing, kind of thing. Showed me stuff. Taught me how to surf, heaps of things.

{GILHOOLEY: A kind of father figure?

This is a new thought for Jared, who shrugs.} *Wilansky throws the file down hard on the desk.*

WILANSKY: You'd do anything he asked?

{JARED: Not anything ...

WILANSKY: Anything to protect him ...

Jared shifts in his seat.}

GILHOOLEY: We've got a problem here, Jared. A girl's dead and no-one did it.

JARED: Heaps of people could have done it!

WILANSKY: Like who?

The question snaps at him. Jared fires back.

JARED: Somebody from the mental hospital! Or ... guys saw this van
with Victorian number plates that night ...
WILANSKY: Strewth, why didn't we think of that, Jared? A total
stranger blows in, finds a girl in distress on a deserted beach, and
for no reason at all murders her, brutally, savagely ...

Wilansky has a coughing fit. Jared is flailing.

JARED: Look ... who says it was murder?
WILANSKY: You're the photographer ...

He sorts through photographs in the file.

... Could you give this a rating on the grunge scale?

*He thrusts a photo under Jared's nose. Jared looks up at him in mute
appeal. He forces it into Jared's grasp. Jared is unable to face the reality
before him.*

[*Out of view*] Does that say 'accident' to you, son?

*Jared's eyes fall on the picture. He blanches, gags, and rises abruptly,
knocking the water jug and shattering a glass as he lurches across the room
to vomit into a bin.*

SCENE 136 EXT. CENTRAL POLICE STATION – THE CITY. DAY.   {114}

*Jared comes out, blinking in the glare. Wilansky watches from a window. {Jared
walks towards the street as though punch-drunk. He steps out from the kerb into
the path of a car. It screeches to a sudden halt. He sees the driver: a young mother,
white with angry fear. There's a schoolkid in the back, and a baby in a safety seat
who howls in fright. Shamefaced, he steps back to the kerb. The woman drives on.
His eyes seem turned inward ...*

SCENE 137 EXT. NEAR THE HEADLAND – BLACKROCK BEACH. NIGHT.

*The dream image, clearer now: Tracy, frail, whimpering, staggers along the beach
towards her death. There's the echo of a small voice ...*
TRACY: Help me ...}

SCENE 138 BLACKROCK BEACH. LATE AFTERNOON.{115, 116, 117}

Jared walks towards the shore-line, still in street clothes. He sees Ricko sitting out the back, riding the swell near the rocks of the point, waiting for a wave. Ricko signals. Jared watches Ricko emerge from the surf, manic under his enforced calm.

RICKO: Aren't you coming out?

Jared shakes his head.

It's dead here. Let's head up the coast.

With a roar Jared lays into him, startling Ricko. The two tussle in the shallows. Jared could throttle Ricko.

Jazza ...

Jared grabs Ricko, hauls him up, yelling in his face.

JARED: You fuckin' lied to me!

RICKO: Bullshit.

JARED: They showed me a photo. How many times, Ricko? How many times did you ...

RICKO: Shut the fuck up!

He pushes Jared away and strides towards the cliff at the end of the beach. Jared catches him, turns him round.

JARED: You meant to do it, didn't you? You knew what you were doing.

RICKO: Well, so did she!

He pulls Jared into the shadow of the cliff.

I was looking for you. And I found her. Stumbling down the beach. She could easy have drowned. She's out of it, asks me to look after her. Tells me I'm a legend, puts her arms round me. 'Hold me', she says. I hold her. Says she feels all right now. She feels more than all right. Asks me to take her home. I said, 'Yeah, I'll take you home, babe, but first things first'. I lay her down on the sand, nice and gentle, but she pushes me off. Okay, she wants it rough, she can have it rough. I get her down again, then she fuckin' bites me, bites me like a fuckin' dog. No bitch does that, mate. Not when they've come on to you like that. She said, 'Hold me' ...

JARED: You meant to do it!

*Over Jared's shoulder Ricko sees a police car parking near the club house.
Two cops get out. (Note: in the finished film the arrival of the police is
treated as a separate scene.)*

RICKO: So you went and dobbed. Like a gutless fuckin' girl.

*He drops his board at the base of the rock and starts to climb the headland.
Above them, on top of Blackrock, sits Ricko's van. Ricko scrambles up.
Jared calls …*

JARED: Don't, Ricko!

*Ricko keeps climbing towards the van. Jared sees the cops run back to the
car. It speeds up the cliff road. Jared clambers up after Ricko, who reaches
the top and disappears. Jared cries out …*

Ricko!

SCENE 139 EXT. THE HEADLAND – BLACKROCK. LATE AFTERNOON.   {118, 119}

*Jared reaches the top, stumbling, breathless. Ricko is running towards the van.
The cop car pulls up beside it … followed by another one. Two cars. Four cops.
Ricko heads for the edge of the cliff. The police run towards him now. Ricko
stands on the edge.*

JARED: No, Ricko!

*The cops are there. Ricko grins a last grin, but it's empty, frightened and
frightening.*

{RICKO: I'll just swim till I hit land.}

*He plunges from sight as the police reach the fence. Two cops drag Jared
back. He wails, restrained by the two cops as Ricko's body is battered
against the rocks. (Note: in the finished film the rocks are treated as a
separate scene.)*

{SCENE 140 INT. THE OPERATING THEATRE, CORRIDOR AND RECOVERY ROOM – THE CITY HOSPITAL. DAY.

*A trolley is wheeled out of the theatre along a fluoro-lit passage, coming to rest in a
curtained alcove. Diane is still unconscious, face pale, hair pulled back.}*

SCENE 141 EXT. A STREET – BLACKROCK. NIGHT.   {120}

A police car passes slowly along the silent street. TV sets flicker in front windows. Lights burn over porches. Several houses are lit up for Christmas. The car stops at the one house which is in total darkness. Jared gets out of the car.

SCENE 142 INT. DIANE'S ROOM – THE KIRBY HOUSE. NIGHT.   {121}

The light from the hall spills across the empty bed. Jared flings himself on the bed. He curls up like a child, clutching his mother's pillow. His hand feels something concealed by it. He pulls out a stack of brochures. He leafs through them, shocked by their titles: Breast Cancer: Before Your Operation; Living With Cancer *...His body on the bed looks frail, curled in the foetal position.*

{SCENE 143 INT. THE PUBLIC WARD – THE CITY HOSPITAL. NIGHT.

On a bed surrounded by curtains which billow softly a night light reveals a motionless form ... Diane. She comes to consciousness. Wincing, she reaches up slowly with her right arm and switches on a small overhead light. The effort exhausts her. She looks at her bandaged wound with its drain, feels pain down her left arm. She raises her right hand, puts it to her right breast, touching, holding it.

SCENE 144 THE SCHOOLYARD. MORNING.

Heavy rain. The Blackos reach the gates in a silent, sombre group. Separate from the boys, Cherie, Shana and Leanne are in a clump at the rear. Tracy's tree lies uprooted. The empty hole is a sodden puddle. Cherie, Shana and Leanne gather round it. Anger surges in their faces.}

SCENE 145 EXT. THE REAR ENCLOSURE – BLACKROCK POLICE STATION. DAY.   {122}

Rain beats down on Blackrock. Through a cyclone wire fence, incongruous in a yard full of police vehicles stands Ricko's van as Cherie clings to the fence, staring at it. There's still rage in her face. She starts to scale the fence. Inside the compound, she leaps to the ground. She strides towards the van, collecting a piece of timber from a garbage bin. She bashes at the van with controlled fury. A policeman comes running out the back door of the station. She ignores his approach and goes on bashing. Another cop comes out. They stare at the girl in her rage, kicking and striking the van ... then move to restrain her. She is sobbing, but flails on, bent on revenge.

SCENE 146 EXT. BLACKROCK BEACH. AFTERNOON. {123}

A procession of Blacko boys carries a surfboard down to the water's edge. The only girl is Tiffany, who holds a bundle of clothes. Jason has a bottle of kero.

SCENE 147 EXT. THE HEADLAND – BLACKROCK. AFTERNOON. {124}

Jared watches the slow procession. He holds one of Ricko's surfing trophies.

SCENE 148 EXT. BLACKROCK BEACH. AFTERNOON. {125}

The board is lowered to the sand. Objects are placed on it. The guys raise the laden surfboard, and bear it into the rippling shallows. Jared reaches the group. Tiffany, crying, takes the trophy and lays it with the rest of Ricko's relics. The burning board is pushed out to sea. Jared hears a whirring noise above. The news helicopter hovers over the beach. Jared stares up at it. The helicopter swoops down, filming. {He walks away in disgust as the flaming board is doused by a wave.}

SCENE 149 INT. THE CORRIDOR– THE CITY HOSPITAL. EVENING. {126}

A TV screens the evening news. Lesley and Ken Warner watch Ricko's funeral. Jared appears with flowers. They stand in a frozen silence.

LESLEY: We'll wait outside.

JARED: Mrs Warner, you stay. I'll come back later.

> *Unnerved by their hostility, he turns away.*

KEN: Just a minute ...

He pulls Jared close, holding him hard. Jared struggles to break free.

You went to Ricketson's send-off.

LESLEY: We saw it on the news.

KEN: Pushing his board out to sea. Like he was some kind of hero. If you weren't Diane's boy ...

Jared breaks free.

JARED: Listen! Tracy had her funeral. Why shouldn't Ricko?

With a roar, Lesley pushes Jared up against a wall, howling, beating at him with her fists.

LESLEY: Animal! Bloody animal!

{*They're in view of the ward. Diane stirs awake.*} *Ken hauls Lesley off, cradling her. Two nurses come running.*

SCENE 150 INT. THE PUBLIC WARD – THE CITY HOSPITAL. EVENING. {127}

Jared goes in, dropping the flowers, which are crushed.

DIANE: G'day, mate.

She catches his gaze falling on her breasts. He looks away, puts the flowers down, sits awkwardly by the bed.

JARED: I'm really sorry. I didn't know.

DIANE: Well, we never had that talk. How long since you had a decent night's sleep? You look like death warmed up.

JARED: You don't look so hot yourself. You feel okay?

DIANE: I'll be right. I will need a bit of help when I get home ...

She sees his embarrassment.

Nothing erky, Jared. Just things I can't manage on my own. Lifting and that ...

He's not looking at her. He mumbles ...

JARED: It's not that, it's just ... I won't be around, probably.

DIANE: How come?

JARED: I'm taking off.

DIANE: Where to? How long for?

He shrugs.

DIANE: Oh, great, mate. Fucking great.

The woman in the next bed looks at Diane, startled. Diane stares back. The woman looks away.

When is it my turn? Jared?

He starts to walk away.

DIANE: It's Ricko, isn't it?

He looks at her, stunned, not understanding.

DIANE: He's off again, is he? This time with his mate. If you go, Jared, that's it.

He stares in anguish and rage, then turns and leaves without looking back.

SCENE 151 EXT. WASTE GROUND BY THE RIVER – BLACKROCK. EVENING.   {128}

Jared wanders across ugly flatlands. No trees on the horizon; only huge abandoned machines.

SCENE 152 INT. THE SUBURBAN GYMNASIUM. DAY.   {129}

Jared peers in to see Len training a young boxer, then slopes away {as a shopkeeper up a ladder hangs Christmas bunting on a nearby awning}.

SCENE 153 EXT. THE HEADLAND – BLACKROCK. NIGHT.{130}

Jared stands where his mate fell to his death. He looks out to sea. But he sees Tracy staggering to her feet as her rapists run off.

SCENE 154 EXT. WASTE GROUND BY THE RIVER – BLACKROCK. DAY.   {131}

A stack of huge concrete tubes destined to be storm-water drains. Jared wakes in one of them. His gear is stacked around him.

SCENE 155 EXT. WASTE GROUND BY THE RIVER – BLACKROCK. NIGHT. {132}

A feeble light glows inside one of the enormous pipes, the only sign of life in this wasteland.

SCENE 156 EXT STREET – BLACKROCK. DAY. {133}

Jared strides down the street past shops decorated for Christmas.

SCENE 157 EXT. WASTELAND DAY {134}

Jared sits in the pipes in the rain.

SCENE 158 EXT OUTSIDE RICKETSON HOUSE – DAY. {135}

Jared buys Ricko's old van from Rick's Dad.

SCENE 159 EXT. WASTE GROUND BY THE RIVER – BLACKROCK. DAY. {136}

Jared still sits motionless. The rain is easing. Rachel holds an umbrella as she stumbles across the rough ground. She peers up into the pipes, finds Jared smoking. He has a can of Coke.

RACHEL: Merry Christmas.

> *He stares at her in silence.*

JARED: Is it Christmas?

> *Jared dangles his legs over the edge of the pipe.*

RACHEL: You going to ask me … up? In?

{JARED: Won't you miss Christmas dinner?

RACHEL: Toby's out on bail. He goes to court soon, January the twentieth. That's all they can talk about. Great Christmas, eh?}

> *He grunts. She dumps her umbrella and clambers up. They sit. He smokes.*

Above: Laurence Breuls as Jared and Jessica Napier as Rachel. Below: Laurence Breuls as Jared. Photos: Elise Lockwood.

{There was this big hole in the exhibition. Half a panel with your name on it. I said that was your statement. Art is process ...

She tries to laugh. It dies.}

Have you missed me?

He nods. She runs a hand through his hair. He doesn't flinch, but doesn't respond.

Are you out of it?

He shakes his head slowly. She takes a drag on his cigarette.

If we're going to break up, shouldn't we have a big fight or something?

She reaches for the soft drink can.

Remember the first day I got the ferry? And Tracy jumped? I thought I could never do that. I did it today, I jumped. {Amazing, the ferry runs on Christmas Day. I got the last one. I don't know how I'll get back. It's a long ride. But I'll stay with you. Chill out, I don't mean forever. Just today. I'll get back somehow.}

She curls up close to him, holding him. His body is inert. She kisses him. He can't respond.

In this expanse of waste ground they seem like two puny figures. One clambers down and slowly walks away.

Jared sees her disappear. He lights another cigarette, his face blank.

SCENE 160 INT./EXT. GLENYS'S CAR – THE KIRBY STREET. DAY. {137}

Glenys approaches the Kirby house, bopping along with Dolly Parton on the radio, down-home accent and all. Cherie is beside her in the front seat.

{GLENYS: 'Here you come again ...'}

Sitting beside Geoff in the back, Diane joins in, nursing a tin can on her lap.

{DIANE: 'Lookin' better than a body has a right to ...'}

Diane sees an old red van parked in the driveway beside the house. Glenys pulls up. Diane starts to get out of the car, still carrying the can.

GEOFF: You want me to come in with you?

Diane shakes her head. Geoff, Glenys and Cherie drive away.

SCENE 161 INT./EXT. THE HALLWAY AND LIVING ROOM – THE KIRBY HOUSE. DAY.   {138}

Diane hurries through the house to find Jared outside the back sliding doors, trying to force them. He sees Diane and yells through the glass.

JARED: You changed the fuckin' locks.

She pulls the doors open.

DIANE: I'm sick of stuff walking.
JARED: My gear. And this is the last time …

She stands stock-still, then ushers him in. She puts the tin can down. He sees it.

Paint-stripper. Going to top yourself?
DIANE: Not just yet.

She follows him …

SCENE 162 INT. JARED'S ROOM – THE KIRBY HOUSE. DAY.{139}

… Into the bare, neat room. The bed is stripped. But the pictures are still up on the walls.

DIANE: Some hoon painted stuff on Tracy's headstone. Ken and Lesley have gone away. Cherie said we have to get it off before they come home.

She watches him pack. Her hands shake as she fumbles to light a cigarette.

JARED: I bet they told you to give up.
DIANE: I have.

The bag is nearly full. His camera sits on the shelf. She holds it out. He ignores it. She puts it down.

Where are you off to?

JARED: None of your business.

DIANE: Up north? The old Ricko route?

He closes the bag.

JARED: Dad was right. You got the rags on every day of the week.

She whacks him hard across the face. He raises his hand. She squares up to him. He grabs his bag and belts towards the back door, pausing to seize the surfboard made by Ricko's hands.

SCENE 163 EXT. THE DRIVEWAY – THE KIRBY HOUSE. DAY.
{140}

He piles the board into the van, gets behind the wheel and turns on the engine. But Diane is standing in front of the van. He eases the van forward, bumps her. She holds her ground.

DIANE: No, mate. I want an apology.

The van bumps her again …

You owe me better than this.

… And again …

You've had a bloody good run with me.

She swings the gates closed.

Too good, I reckon.

He gets out of the van, opens the gates, but as he piles back in the driver's seat, she opens the passenger door and gets in.

JARED: I'm out of here …

He revs the engine.

DIANE: It's okay, mate. I've got all day. I'm here till you apologise.

JARED: You'll wait a fuckin' long time.

He drives away down the street in silence.

{SCENE 164 EXT. THE ROAD TO BLACKROCK WHARF. DAY.

Waste ground. Billboards. One of them advertises the new Body Count *campaign: beautiful female torsos in underwear. There's a flicker of recognition in Jared's eyes. He drives at speed, handling the cranky gears like a veteran.*

DIANE: You need a haircut.
JARED: You need a brick in your mouth.

> *He's retracing the route of Ricko's arrival. The huge span of the bridge is ahead, beyond it the steelworks and dockyards.*

SCENE 165 EXT. THE BRIDGE TO BLACKROCK. DAY.

The van crests the bridge again like a wave. This time, the wave will break the other way.}

SCENE 166 INT./EXT. RICKO'S VAN –THE BRIDGE TO BLACKROCK. DAY. {141}

They're higher than they've been. The city is to one side, the docklands and steelworks to the other.

DIANE: You going for good?

> *He says nothing.*

Christ, I'm not the fucking cops. Are you ever coming back?

> *He shakes his head. He pulls up beside the road. They seem to be suspended in air, the skyline encroaching on either side.*

JARED: Okay. I was out of line. I'm sorry. You happy? Now you can get out.

> *She has a hand on the door. She's about to open it and go.*

DIANE: Will you do me a favour? Write me a letter one day? Tell me what happened to you? 'Cause ... I lost you that night, didn't I? That's like losing a part of myself.

> *His eyes fall towards her breasts. He looks up. She meets his gaze.*

Mother and son don't touch.

I owe you an apology, too. Ever since that night, I was half-thinking … it might have been you … that did it. I'm sorry, son.

She tries to smile. She opens the door. He puts a hand on her arm. He tries to speak. The words are a croak.

JARED: Mum … listen … It was my fault.

He looks out the window towards the bridge. Her hand is poised on the door-handle.

That night … I was sitting up on the rock, having a smoke and a think … Moon on the water and all that. I saw them down on the beach, doing it to her. I heard them, I heard her crying. They pissed off. She went down the beach, little tiny voice, calling for help. Little bell ringing round her neck. I turned and ran the other way. I could have gone down there any time, I could have stopped them. Even after, I could have taken her home. Only I wouldn't. I didn't.

She can't hide her shock and distress.

DIANE: Why?

He looks down to the water … across to the docks.

JARED: If I knew, I mightn't feel like such a piece of shit.
DIANE: Why do you think?
JARED: Guys are …

He can't finish the thought. He can't look at her. He looks out across this steel city.

You got mates, they're your mates. That's all you got. That's the way it is.
DIANE: And you let a girl die …

She gets out of the van, leaving the door open. He watches her go, leans over, closes the passenger door and drives away.

SCENE 167 EXT. THE BRIDGE TO BLACKROCK. DAY.   {142}

Diane sees Ricko's van disappear down the other side of the bridge. She turns and hurries back towards the town, biting her lip. Her tears begin to flow. She hurries on, not looking back, as the van gets smaller in the distance. When she's halfway down the slope of the bridge, the van has gone.

SCENE 168 EXT. BLACKROCK CEMETERY. DAY. {143}

A little later. Diane and Cherie work at Tracy's new headstone with solvent and scrubbing brushes. Diane stops. Her left arm is still stiff. She kneads it. Over the top of the stone, a figure appears at the gate. Cherie first notices Jared walking slowly towards the stone. Then Diane sees him. They watch his gaze fall on the headstone, see the shame and shock in his eyes. 'SLUT' is daubed across it in red. Cherie trembles. She and Jared survey one another warily. Then she goes back to work. Diane rests her sore arm. Jared takes her scrubbing brush. Diane watches Jared and Cherie work at cleaning the headstone in the cemetery on a cliff overlooking the rolling ocean on this placid summer day.

{SCENE 169 EXT. THE BRIDGE TO BLACKROCK. SUNSET.

The battered red van stands by the side of the road. Cars drive past it as the sun sets behind the industrial skyline.}

Film End Credits

CAST
Jared LAURENCE BREULS/ Diane LINDA CROPPER/ Ricko
SIMON LYNDON/ Rachel JESSICA NAPIER/Tracy BOYANA
NOVAKOVIC/ Det Sgt Wilansky CHRIS HAYWOOD/ Det.
Gilhooley ESSIE DAVIS/ Cherie REBECCA SMART/ Tiffany
JUSTINE CLARKE/ Lesley Warner JEANETTE CRONIN/ Ken
Warner DAVID FIELD/ Glenys SHAYNE FRANCIS/ Toby
HEATH LEDGER / Stewart Ackland GEOFF MORELL/ Len Kirby
JOHN HOWARD/ Geoff JOHN O'HARE / Doctor KATE SHEIL/
Davo BRENDAN DONOGHUE/ Jason CAMERON NUGENT/
Scottie JADE GATT/ Kemel GEORGE BASHA/ Leanne NICHOLE
AVRAMIDIS/ Shana LEEANNA WALSMAN/ Leesha KELLIE
BRIGHT/ Deck-hand PHILIP DODD/ Interviewer (Female) LUCIA
MASTRANTONE/ Interviewer (Male) BRIAN MEEGAN/ Blackrock
boy DANIEL CARLIN/ Blackrock girl SOPHIE WIESNER/ Jason's
Mate TYSON McCONKEY/ Marian Ackland JULIE HASELER/ Mr
Kamen RITCHIE SINGER/ Mr Ayoub STAVROS ECONOMIDIS/
Mrs Ayoub GINA BORTOLIN/ Bloke in Gym DOUGLAS
HEDGE/ Principal HAROLD HOPKINS/ Ricko's Dad PAUL
JONES/ Rhonda KIM LEWIS/ Stan MIKEY ROBBINS/ Teacher
SACHA HORLER/ Town Guy JOHNATHAN DEVOY/ Shana's
Mother DENISE KIRBY/ Photographer's Assistant ALVARO
MARQUES/ Gary PIP BRANSON/ Band SIDEWINDER/
Helicopter Cameraman PHIL MOBBS/ Surfer #1 AARON CARTER/
Surfer #2 MARK STANBOROUGH/ Uniformed Cop JULIE GRAY/
Stunt Police Driver TONY LYNCH/ Tracey's Stunt Double GILLIAN
STRATHAM/ Stunt Driver PAUL DOYLE/ Stunt Police Driver
KATHY McMORROW/ Ricko's Stunt Double NIGEL HARBACH/
Jared's Stunt Double NASH EDGERTON/ Surfing Double DANIEL
THOMSON

CREW
Director STEVE VIDLER/ Producer DAVID ELFICK/ Screenplay
NICK ENRIGHT/ Original Score STEVE KILBEY/ Script Editor

STEVE VIDLER/ Casting CHRISTINE KING, LIZ MULLINAR/ Production Manager CATHERINE KNAPMAN/ Production Coordinator LIBBY SHARPE/ Production Secretary HELEN LINTHORNE/ Extras Casting KATE FINSTERER/ Producer's Assistant VALERIE WILLIAMS/ Production Runner ALICE LANAGAN/ Production Accountant BELLE EDER/ Accounts Assistant STUART McPHEE/ 1st Assistant Director CHARLES ROTHERHAM/ 2nd Assistant Director KAREN MAHOOD/ 3rd Assistant Director ANDREW POWER/ Continuity CARMEL TORCASIO/ Locations Manager ROBIN CLIFTON/ Unit Manager AUBREY TREDGET/ Unit Assistant SHANE NAYLOR/ Unit Assistant PAUL NAYLOR/ Additional AD JEREMY SEDLEY/ Rushes Driver ED PETTY/ Second Unit Director DAVID ELFICK/ Second Unit DOP CALUM McFARLANE/ Second Unit Focus Puller FRANK FLICK/ Water Sequences GEORGE GREENOUGH MARK THOMSON/ Director of Photography & Camera Operator MARTIN McGRATH ACS/ Focus Puller KATRINA CROOK/ Clapper Loader REBECCA STEELE/ Gaffer DAVID PARKINSON/ Best Boy GREG RAWSON/ 3rd Electrics SCOTT COPELAND/ 4th Electrics MANFRED HNILICA/ Grip BRETT McDOWELL/ Assistant Grip TIM DUGGAN/ Sound Designer ANDREW PLAIN/ Sound Recordist GUNTIS SICS/ Boom Operator MICHAEL TAYLOR/ Art Director SAM RICKARD/ Art Department Coordinator SANDRA (HEIDI) OOSTERMAN/ Set Decorator GLEN W. JOHNSON/ Props Buyer ADAM SLATER/ Standby Props GEORGE ZAMMIT/ Props Buyer SAM COOK/ Sets and Staging MEGADECK/ Vehicle Co-ordinator TIM PARRY/ Storyboard Artist ROBERT ALCOCK/ Scenic Artist PETA BLACK

PRODUCTION

Costume Designer DAVID McKAY/ Costume Supervisor JACKLINE SASSINE/ Costume Assistant SARA MATHERS/ Standby Wardrobe GABRIELLE DUNN/ Makeup/Hair Supervisor JAN (ZIGGY) ZEIGENBEIN/ Makeup/Hair Assistant BEC TAYLOR/ Stunt Co-ordinator ROCKY McDONALD/ Safety Officer KERRY BLAKEMAN/ Nurse MANDY LING/ Caterer RED STAR CATERING, EAT AND SHOOT THROUGH/ Editor FRANS VANDENBURG/ Assistant Editor PETER SKARRATT/ Dialogue Editor KARIN WHITTINGTON/ Dialogue Assistant NICHOLAS BRESLIN/ Dialogue Editor BRENT BURGE/ Dialogue Assistant

DELIA MCCARTHY/ Sound FX Editor JANE PATERSON/ Sound FX Assistant NADA MIKAS/ Sound Mixer GETHIN CREAGH/ Sound Mixer MARTIN OSWIN/ Editing Room and Post Production Facilities SPECTRUM FILMS/ Mixing Facility SOUNDFIRM/ Film Laboratory ATLAB/ Laboratory Liaison IAN RUSSELL/ Negative Matcher KAREN PSALTIS/ Grader ARTHUR CAMBRIDGE/ Tape House DIGITAL PICTURES/ Publicity EDWINA STUART, ONE GLOBE PROMOTIONS/ Stills Photographer ELISE LOCKWOOD/ Titles Design and Production ANIMAL LOGIC/ Designer DEBORAH McNAMARA/ Domino Operator SIMON CARR/ Film Technician CHRIS SWINBANKS/ Producer MELANIE RITCHIE/ Film Stock KODAK (AUSTRALASIA)/ Camera equipment SAMUELSONS/ Unit Vehicles EMPIRE FILM SERVICES/ Unit Truck UNIT ONE FILM UNIT/ Helicopter HELICRUISE AIR SERVICES/ Insurance H.W. WOOD AUSTRALIA/ Completion Guarantor FILM FINANCES INC/ Solicitor HART AND SPIRA, NINA STEVENSON.

The stage play BLACKROCK was developed and financed by the Sydney Theatre Company.
Developed and produced with the assistance of the New South Wales Film and Television Office, Sydney Australia.
Financed by the Australian Film Finance Corporation.
International Sales Beyond Films.
Produced in association with PolyGram Filmed Entertainment.
Music Supervisor ROGER GRIERSON, POLYGRAM MUSIC PUBLISHING. Original Music by Steve Kilbey under license from PolyGram Music Publishing Australia Pty Limited. Soundtrack available on Mercury Records

Screenplays from Currency Press

Love Serenade
Shirley Barrett

Spotswood
Max Dann and
Andrew Knight

Bad Boy Bubby
Rolf de Heer

Children of the Revolution
Peter Duncan

*The Adventures of Priscilla,
Queen of the Desert*
Stephan Elliott

Muriel's Wedding
P.J. Hogan

Strictly Ballroom
Baz Luhrmann
and Craig Pearce

Cosi, the screenplay
Louis Nowra

Dead Heart, the screenplay
Nick Parsons

Dingo
Marc Rosenberg

Angel Baby
Michael Rymer

The Sum of Us
David Stevens

All inquiries to:

Currency Press
PO Box 452, Paddington NSW 2021
Tel: 61 (0)2 9332 1399   Fax: 62 (0)2 9332 3848
e-mail: currency@magna.com.au
Website: http://www.currency.com.au